KEY to
Stress-Free Living

Stress Management for Wellness

Dr. Jyotsna Codaty

Published by:

F-2/16, Ansari Road, Daryaganj, New Delhi-110002
011-23240026, 011-23240027 • *Fax:* 011-23240028
Email: info@vspublishers.com • *Website:* www.vspublishers.com

Branch : Hyderabad
5-1-707/1, Brij Bhawan (Beside Central Bank of India Lane)
Bank Street, Koti, Hyderabad - 500 095.
040-24737290.
E-mail: vspublishershyd@gmail.com

Follow us on:

For any assistance sms **VSPUB** to **56161**
All books available at **www.vspublishers.com**

© Copyright: V&S PUBLISHERS
ISBN 978-93-814489-9-1
Edition 2013

The Copyright of this book, as well as all matter contained herein (including illustrations) rests with the Publishers. No person shall copy the name of the book, its title design, matter and illustrations in any form and in any language, totally or partially or in any distorted form. Anybody doing so shall face legal action and will be responsible for damages.

Printed at : Param Offseters, Okhla, New Delhi-110020

DEDICATION

This book is dedicated to my family who put up with me in my times of stress, to my many friends who helped me at every step and to my readers who I hope, will SMILE!

CONTENTS

Preface 7
1. The Beginning 9
2. Types of Stress 14
3. The Stages of Stress 16
4. Causes of Stress 25
5. Coping with Stress 31
6. Recognising Stress 40
7. Combatting Stress 45
8. Finding the Time 64
9. Stress and Children 70
10. Stress and Indian Women 83
11. Overseas Stress 93
12. Stress and Retirement 104
13. Stress and Superstition 115
14. Stress at Workplace 119
15. Stress and your Financial Portfolio ... 123
16. Stress between Husband and Wife ... 126
17. Stress and Illness 130
18. Techniques to bust your stress 133

PREFACE

This book is a happy book.

This book is about enjoying life.

This book is about making choices.

At the same time, it is important to acknowledge that not all of lifes outcomes are chosen. The attempt is to make clear what people can control and what they cannot.

The theme of this book is:
That a persons state of health is, to a great extent, his own responsibility.

To create awareness, so that lifestyle choices can be made.

To emphasise that problems are not common to all individuals, as the reactions to them are not. Obviously, the solutions are a matter of choice. There are no definite black or white areas.

The book is positive; its emphasis is on what to do and not so much on what not to do.

—**Dr. Jyotsna Codaty**

Chapter 1
The Beginning

Stress initially, was used in the biological context in the beginning of the 20th Century. Signs of stress may be cognitive, emotional, physical or behaviour that include poor judgement, negative outlook in general, excessive worry, change of mood, irritation while working, agitation, problem in relaxing, feeling isolated, abnormal heartbeat, eating too much or not enough withdrawal from society, avoiding responsibilities, increased consumption of alcohol or drugs, habits showing nervousness, nail biting, lack of concentration, forgetfulness, indigestion, loss of appetite, weight loss or weight gain, and headache with constant fatique.

There was a time long age when people were happy most of the time. They had a little land, they made their own clothes, hunted their own food and built their own houses depending on where they lived. They found their life partners, had children, and the children grew up doing much the same as their parents did.

Even then, they had their own share of problems. They had wild animals to ward off, they were concerned about

being human, they had their quarrels. Some were sorted out, some ended by drawing blood. They had invaders to

leisure, they lived and died without too much ado.

Down the centuries, society built its walls and its dogma around man. Life followed set patterns. The houses got better, the clothes got finer. The food was cooked to established standards, a social hierarchy was set up, animals were harnessed for work in fields and to draw carriages. Some were even domesticated as man's best friend. Simple tools were crafted, and men and women continued to live at a leisurely pace.

There were floods and fires and invaders to fight and fob off. There was money to earn, clothes and houses to buy, and being human, there were fights and conflicts—for land, for money and for women. Thus, along with leisure they had to go through a lot of tough manual labour that made man tired and yet fulfilled at the end of the day. Women too had plenty to do around the house, looking after the animals, collecting firewood and cooking for large families.

Today, we have our houses, we have our cars, we have our computers, and we have our paraphrenalia of gadgetry to help us get things done. We have our organisers to remind us what we have to get done today. We no longer fight wars, our governments do that for us, and we have television and the media to tell us what is happening around the world. And we have to fight a system that is so flawed that most of our time goes, if not fighting it, then at least talking about it. And we have our doctors that tell us we need to relax, and ask us, are you under stress? And we pay money to teachers/doctors/gurus to tell us how to get rid of stress.

We are stressed out while going to sleep. We are stressed out getting up, we are stressed out from not eating properly, we are stressed out from eating the wrong things, we are stressed out about our children, or so stressed that we cannot have children. We are stressed out searching for better jobs, or stressed out from keeping our job. We are stressed out from not having proper help at home, or we are stressed out trying to find better ones, and we are so stressed out that even our three-year-old child is stressed out and needs therapy!

"Stop the world. I want to get off!"

Did you feel like shouting these words aloud, or at least saying them to yourself? Better still, did the pace of today's world tempt you to be like a farmer, who rested beside the brook singing a song? His simple life that brought him so much tranquility is definitely worth emulating.

> *Mine be a cot beside the hill;*
> *A bee-hive's hum shall soothe my ear;*
> *A willowy brook that turns the mill,*
> *With many a fall shall linger near.*
> *The swallow, oft, beneath my thatch*
> *Shall twitter from her clay built nest;*
> *Oft shall the pilgrim lift the latch,*
> *And share my meal, a welcome guest.*
> *Around my ivied porch shall spring*
> *Each fragrant flower that drinks the dew;*
> *And Lucy, at her wheel, shall sing*
> *In russet gown and apron blue.*
> *The village church among the trees,*
> *Where first our marriage vows were given,*
> *With merry peals shall swell the breeze*
> *And point with taper spire to Heaven.*
>
> —S. Rogers

I wish life were that simple, a matter of buying a cottage down the hill with a brook flowing beside and your wife humming a song! Somewhere along the way, we got so entangled with the world around us that we changed. Changed so much that our life's goals appear to have altered to such an extent that we seem to be living simply. We have changed to an actively consumerist and existentialist society.

Early man was scared of wild animals and mostly died while hunting. As time passed other living forms, albeit much smaller than him in size, began to get the better of him. He began to fall ill with different diseases caused by various bacteria. Today, we are again on the verge of victory; with our intelligence and effort, we have conquered many of them and rid the world of nearly most of them. Sadly, we became prey to illnesses of our own making, illnesses of our own lifestyle, and illnesses caused by our own wrong choices.

Metaphorically running to keep pace with our own internal demons, to foist on our psyche, our ever-increasing ambitions and desires, all in the name of keeping pace with the times, and rationalising that in today's competitive world there is no place for complacence.

- Do we not owe ourselves some answers before we begin to understand the so-called whims of today's living patterns?
- Do we not owe ourselves simple plain good health?
- Do we not owe ourselves a sense of self-esteem?
- Do we not owe ourselves the right to choose?
- Do we not owe ourselves a stress-free life?

To realise the chaos caused by our attitude, I will start with some statistics. Not the most exciting of beginnings, but a point from where we get a good perspective of the issues concerned. The primary causes of disease and death in the last century and the present one have been as follows:

20th Century	21st Century
Tuberculosis	Heart disease
Pneumonia	Cancer
Stroke	Accidents
Infectious diseases	Suicide
Kidney diseases	Diabetes Substance abuse Lung disease Stroke AIDS

You will notice that the profile of mortality and morbidity has totally changed in the past century from what was beyond one's control to what seems to be a matter of wrong choices. Those of you who were born in the 50's or later, will recognise a certain change in the illness patterns and also in people's reactions to them. In those days, a heart attack was something that happened in the mid or early fifties and there was very little to be done. In the 70's, it became a disease afflicting 40-year-olds, and by the time we entered 80's, people started coming home from foreign countries with a new set of arteries. This did not reduce the incidence of heart attack. Though the victims these days are only in their mid 30's, they have pretty good chance to be hit by stress syndrome.

The same goes for the increasing number of cancers, and the newer diseases like AIDS. In the new millennium though, we seem to be seeing some light at the end of the tunnel.

A wave of awareness has commenced, and its effect will spread. The era of choices has begun!

To begin to sort out what is troubling us, it is essential to first define the state of well-being.

And we will begin this quest with a voyage of self discovery,

A voyage where we will search for what we really want from life,

A voyage to identify the real new you.

Chapter 2
Types of Stress

In general, a person experiences different types of stress. These range from personal, to stress at workplace, and strained relationships in the family, among others. Stress

after an event like an accident, stress arising out of neighbourhood problems, or any political news.

into following four main categories of stress:

1. Eustress
You must have felt:

> Thrilled and excited while watching a horror movie.
> Excited when you won a game or prize.

> Happiness in accomplishing a challange.
> Happy and excited when you went for a holiday.

All these feelings are called good stress. Positive stress makes us feel good, thereby exerting a healthy effect. Such

this kind of stress occurs only for a short period of time. Eustress gives a person the ability to generate optimum output by performing his best. This is also called curative stress.

2. Distress
Looking at both sides of life, there is positive and negative stress, also known as good or bad stress, respectively.

These kinds of stress are the opposites of Eustress and collectively are called Distress. It is a negative stress caused by adverse events that influence a person's ability to cope. Some of the following events lead to distress:

- Death of someone you love.
- Chronic illness.
- Financial crisis.
- Strained relationships.
- Responsibility of heavy workload.

Acute stress and chronic stress are the two classifications of distress. While the former is short lived, the latter is usually prolonged in nature.

3. Hyperstress

When a person is pushed beyond what one can handle, the resulting experience is called hyperstress. It comes from being overworked. When someone is hyperstressed, even little things can trigger a strong emotional response. The following people are most likely to be affected by hypertension:

- Those who constantly have financial difficulties.
- Mothers who have to look after their office work along with other family commitments.
- Vendors also are continuously under tension of selling.
- People working in a fast-paced environment.
- Salesmen travelling during the night and working during the day.

4. Hypostress

Hypostress is directly opposite to hyperstress. Hypostress is experienced by people who constantly feel bored, such as a factory worker performing the same task over and over again. Here the feelings of restlessness and a lack of inspiration prevails.

Chapter 3
The Stages of Stress

Man must know how to live in good terms with himself, how to manage and control and sometimes improve himself. "Make it thy business to know thyself,"

lesson in the world."

What exactly is health?
Health is a state of complete physical, mental and social well-being and not merely the absence of disease and

Just being free from disease is not enough. One needs to include emotional, interpersonal, social, intellectual and spiritual well-being.

We must take the responsibility on ourselves to stay healthy. To keep well, and to the extent possible, being in control of our own little world.

Is there something holding us back from this endeavour and preventing us from being in control of situations? This niggling, nagging demon is Stress. While it is very common to blame all ills on stress, do we even realise what exactly stress is?

The situation can be anything, from a life-threatening illness to merely being late for work, from losing a loved one to a school admission, from uprooting yourself from known surroundings to a quarrel in the family.

No two individuals react to the same stress in the same way, or even regard the same situation as a stressful event.

Stress is not synonymous with nervous tension or anxiety, as is commonly believed. Stress has its good points, and an optimum level provides the means to express talents and energies and pursue happiness. The important thing to remember is that stress is normal and essential.

Is stress bad?

No. In fact, stress is a *motivating factor*. It is needed to perform. It is just that continuous and accumulating stress is detrimental to health.

Before we begin to discuss what exactly are the body's responses to stress, let us start with the attitude that a little bit of tension, a little bit of anxiety, in short, a little bit of stress is a good and essential requisite for our well-being.

Let me introduce you to this family that is so quintessentially Indian. Perhaps in this family, we will identify a little of someone we know, or someone we deal with every day; we may even identify ourself.

Like in all families sagas, we have the grandfather Mr. Surendranath and we have his wife, Kamala. Surendranath retired as a head clerk from a government office, while Kamala stayed at home and looked after the children. They have three offsprings. Vijay, the eldest, works as a scientist in a government office and is married to Sarita, a computer programmer. They have two little kids, a boy aged six, and a girl aged four. Surendranth's daughter Anita is a lecturer in a college, and was recently married to Gopal, an engineer working with a private firm in the same town. The youngest boy Ramesh dreamt of going to medical college, but not having made the grade, had to give up the idea as his parents did not have the financial resources to send him to a private college. He is now training to be a microbiologist, but remains somewhat disgruntled that his parents found the money to pay for Anita's marriage, but refused his request to pay for tuition to a private medical college.

All of them live in a modest house that is the ancestral property of Surendranath. This house is mortgaged to the bank to raise a loan for Anita's marriage. Vijay and Sarita contribute to the running of the house, and occasionally there is grumbling in the family that they should also help in paying off the loan as eventually, they would be the beneficiaries of Surendranath's estate. Sarita and her mother-in-law get along reasonably well most of the time. Sarita is grateful that she does not have the problems of her colleagues when it comes to minding the children, but she occasionally differs from her mother-in-law in various aspects of bringing up children. There is some conflict whenever she splurges on clothes and some small pieces of jewellery. The elders feel that a little thrift can help in paying off the loan.

Anita visits her parents over the weekend with her husband. While it was initially welcomed, Sarita feels this is as an intrusion into her time and space, while the elders feel it is a pleasure, and that Sarita should go out of her way to entertain her sister-in-law and her husband. Sarita is bad-tempered over the weekend, and complains to her husband Vijay that all this makes for extra work and as a career woman, she needs some rest too. Vijay is uncomfortable telling this to his parents, and on an odd occasion he tried to, was fobbed off by the reply, 'don't be a hen-pecked husband. More often than not Vijay is helpless, and Sarita is angry with him. This reflects on the children too, with the grandmother complaining that she does not get enough rest. Sarita says she is helpless.

Ramesh adds his little bit by being demanding in terms of his needs like good clothes and fancy dishes to eat. He takes every opportunity to remind his siblings that he has been treated in a step-motherly fashion.

So life goes on, with its little problems and small arguments. In this apparently happy family, there is a little tension, a little maladjustment and few major conflicts. Every now and then, we will keep getting back to them to understand the process of stress.

With this story in the background, let us look at what happens when we encounter a stressful situation.

One can respond with one, two or all of the following sequences of events. All of them take place in our body for varying lengths of time; this generally determines our attitude to the situation.

Stage 1: Mobilisation of energy

When the person encounters a stressful situation—let us call it a *"stressor"*—all body activity increases. It literally goes into high gear. Commonly, it is called a "fight or flight" response. We commonly use the phrase, "pumping of adrenaline". Scientifically, this is what exactly happens. The body produces increased quantities of the hormone adrenaline that gives the body extra momentum.

This is an essential and favourable reaction to any *stressor*. The situation could be as simple as a dog chasing you. The extra adrenaline gives you that extra

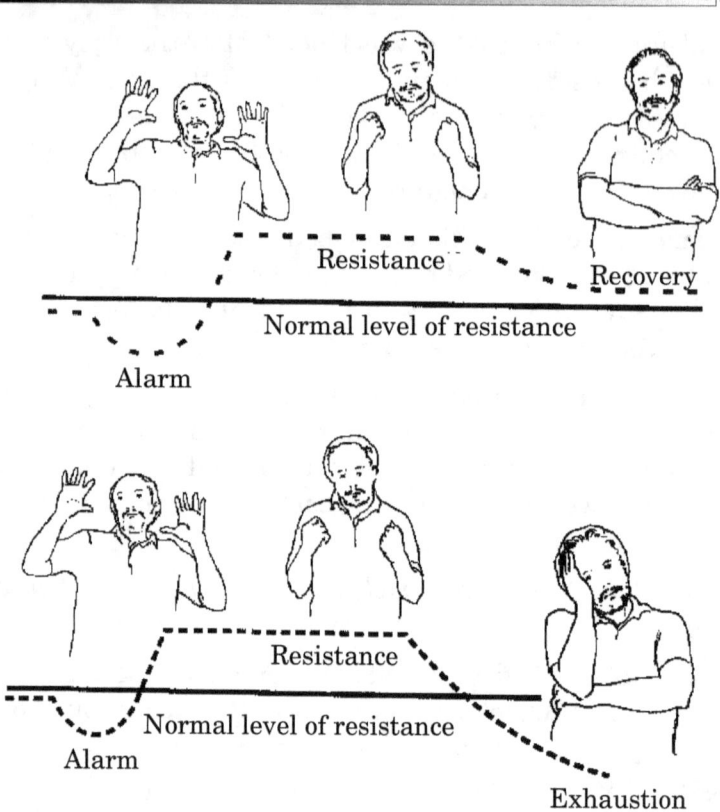

burst of speed to rally and run from the situation. It is not necessary that this happens only in unfavourable situations. Suppose Sarita's son is about to participate in a race, the mixed emotions of anxiety, desire to win the challenge, all these add up to tell the body that a *stressor* lies ahead, and the body responds by giving it a spurt of adrenaline—enough to run, and maybe win the race.

What happens in the first phase is called the good stress. Technically, it is called *primary stress*.

What you feel during this adrenaline rush is—

Your heart is beating much faster than it does normally, and your palms are sweaty.

Don't you recollect this entire scenario happening when you are about to face an interview, or take an examination, or maybe when you are about to be interviewed by a visa officer or even called by your boss to explain something?

There is a slight variant to this, *secondary stress,* where you know that the event is due to happen, you want it to happen, but you are all the same tense about it. Some common examples are, just before your wedding, or a distant journey, or you are off on a foreign assignment leaving your family for the first time, or when you know you or your loved one needs an operation and you are tense. This reflects in your body in the form of—

- Loss of appetite
- Rapid breathing
- Increased heart rate and blood pressure
- Sweating

Anita probably felt all this just before her wedding, as would have Surendranath. He was tensed about arranging the finances, but he was also happy that his daughter was getting married. This form of stress takes a little longer to abate, and here the mind is aware that you are tensed about an upcoming situation that you are willingly undertaking. In spite of your willingness, the very nature of the event puts some amount of stress on your psyche and over a period of time, causes symptoms like loss of appetite, etc.

This initial, mobilisation of energy phase is transient, and soon gets over.

It ends with the completion of the event that caused the stress.

Stage 2: Exhaustion or consuming energy

We concluded that the first stage would end with the

conclusion of the event, be it an examination, race or operation. What happens if the situation is prolonged, or the end unsatisfactory? Suppose you did not fare well in the interview, and are very unsure of the outcome. Or the athlete lost the race, and is worried about the consequences of losing.

Maybe Ramesh feels a sense of dejection that he could not go to medical college. He has not been able to adjust to his new career even though it is three years since he started this course. Surendranath also occasionally feels the tension of the loan he has taken for Anita's wedding. Recently, he developed high blood pressure and is now under treatment. His wife Kamala is sometimes upset about the little upsets in the family, and feels everyone is taking her for granted. She does not yet know it, but she is becoming a victim of stress.

Anita and Sarita's problems can be categorised as in the second stage, and some honest introspection on both their parts can prevent the escalating tension in the family. Particularly, there is potential here for Vijay to become a stressed-out person, apart from Sarita who is already feeling the tension.

If a sincere attempt is made to correct the behavioural pattern at this point by firstly realising that a problem exists, and with introspection and dialogue coming to an agreeable solution, they can happily come back to stage one, else they retain the potential to proceed on to stage three, from where the journey to normality becomes that much more difficult.

When there is no escape from stage one, the body begins to release stored sugars and fats, using up its reserves. It is literally emptying out its storehouse to meet the continued stress situation. The body begins to feel:

- Tired and fatigued
- Pressurised
- Increase in anxiety
- Memory loss

Stage 3: Depletion of energy

When an individual fails to take corrective action sometime during stage two, the body more or less uses up all its reserves. To illustrate, let us take the case of the sports person who failed to win a race. He is worried about the repercussions it will have on his career. He lets the issue dominate his thought process to such an extent, that he even loses focus on his routine training. Expectedly, his performance deteriorates, and this in turn, aggravates his anxiety, and builds on his stress levels. Or take the case of the executive who is unsure of his performance in an interview. His anxiety persists, and bothers him to such an extent that he is unable to take constructive steps. When this continues to happen over a prolonged period of time, it leads to:

- Heart diseases
- High blood pressure
- Stomach ulcers
- Personality changes
- Errors in judgement

At the end of it, the affable athlete and the smiling executive undergo so much change in temperament that they become Mr. Grumble and Mr. Grouch.

This seems to be the stage where Ramesh is now. He is not willing to reconcile to his being unable to join medical college, and bears some hostility to others for the situation.

Surendranath also is in a state of tension about repaying the loan, and that his elder son, Vijay, has not been particularly cooperative in helping out. He did hope that both Vijay and his wife, Sarita, would help. Now, it has become a source of worry, and with his high blood pressure, he is further worried that after his demise, his wife would find the going tough.

Sarita and Vijay may soon join this segment if they do not take corrective steps as soon as possible.

Chapter 4
Causes of Stress

Let us examine the causes of stress. With most things, the

be pointed out. Ask any person known to you as to what they consider to be *stressors*, and nine out of ten times, the answers will be events like the loss of a loved one,

problems, major changes in life like change of place of residence as in moving from one city to another, divorce, family tensions, so on and so forth. These are called life events and are correctly labelled even by the most naive person as *stressors*. Surendranath's house loan and his daughter's wedding fall under this category, as also Ramesh's failure to make it to the course of his choice.

The other types of *stressors* are called
These are the culprits that cause our body to face the threat of aggression day in and day out. We do not even realise it. These types of events have become such an integral part of our daily life in India that we have accepted them as a part of living. It is a moot question whether our body and psyche have accepted them with as much aplomb as we think our mind has accepted it. Driving to work in rush hour, waiting for most things that are beyond our comprehension, like to pay a telephone bill or book and reserve a railway ticket, deadlines to meet in the office, chronic absenteeism of colleagues that unexpectedly adds to your workload, conflict in personal lives as in daily quarrels between

members of the family over minor issues. A major part of this category figures conflict between sisters-in-law, conflict between mother-in-law and daughter-in-law, and in some cases, conflict between neighbours.

Minor issues like the irregularity of household help, water shortage, tension over the outcome of the examination of children as young as class one and two, extreme competitiveness where children are concerned, add to the stress. I have intentionally listed a large number of seemingly innocuous issues to highlight the cumulative effect of these little things in causing problems over a long period of time. All the perceived problems of Surendranath's family seem to fall under this category.

Where stress is concerned, it is a process that builds up. Every little thing adds up.

We have now accepted that a number of major and minor issues cause stress in our daily lives. Having come this far, how do we know that our body is reacting unfavourably? Some of the earliest giveaways of detecting stress are:

- General irritability
- Sleeplessness
- Headaches
- Indigestion
- Pain in the neck
- High Blood Pressure leading to various heart problems
- Accident proneness
- Trembling
- Change in appetite and sleep habits
- Depression

Let us now indulge in a small self-assessment exercise to establish the stress index.

Here are a few questions that you should answer spontaneously.

- Do you get angry easily?
- Do you set unrealistic goals for yourself and for the people working with/under you or your family members?
- Do you do everything yourself?
- Do you act rude very often?
- Do you make a big issue of everything?
- Do you avoid people whose ideas are different from yours?
- Do you keep everything bottled up inside you?
- Do you never see humour in any situation?
- Do you believe that there is only one correct way of doing anything; that there is no possibility of alternatives?
- Do you gossip a lot?
- Do you complain of the past often?
- Do you race through the day everyday?
- Do you neglect exercise/physical activity?
- Do you neglect your diet?
- Do you take sleeping pills?

Award 1 mark for each "No" and 2 marks for each "Yes". If you have scored 16 or less, you are in good control of your life, and do not let the little bothers of life hassle you.

If you have scored anything between 16 and 22, you need to think over things a bit, and might want to take some corrective steps.

Anything more than 22, and you really need to introspect and might even need to consider taking professional help.

During my clinical practice, many patients have walked in complaining of various aches and pains. When allowed to talk openly and freely, they moret often come out with some totally unrelated family or job-related problem. This is generally introduced as a matter of conversation.

When an upfront question is asked if the person is under any undue stress, the answer generally is in the negative. The person is not trying to hide something, though occasionally even that may happen. He just does not perceive that "something" as a special problem that may be reflecting in his general feeling of being "unwell". I will illustrate with a few common examples to highlight situations that have the potential of being a *stressor*. Each individual is the best judge of what are the situations that upset him.

Situation 1: Kumar is an executive who is climbing up the corporate ladder quickly. He is intelligent and ambitious. This morning he got up late, and was trying to get his things in order when his wife told him that she needs to be dropped off at work. Kumar is upset at this last minute change of plans. He rushes, and unfortunately the usual traffic snarls further upset him. He has an important presentation, and he is quite tense about this. Fortunately, he does reach office in time, the presentation goes off well, and he bags another assignment.

Situation 2: Sarla is a housewife. She lives with her in-laws. Most often things move smoothly in the house without friction, but at times, Sarla and her mother-in-law differ in their views about bringing up children. The elder lady feels that undue fuss is made of every little thing while she coped well enough with four kids of her own. Sarla does not agree. She feels that the grandparents unduly pamper her son, and the child needs a little bit of discipline, while they feel that being mischievous is the prerogative of the youngster. Sarla cannot openly defy them, though she tries to say that times have changed.

Situation 3: Satish is an employee in a factory. He is careful with his finances, and very cautious about making financial decisions. His wife Seema feels he is unduly cautious. After all, his colleagues do spend on the occasional outing and for all festivals. She feels deprived and tends to nag. Sometimes, tempers flare up, and heated words are exchanged.

Situation 4: Mohan and Sunita have placed great hopes on their son Rajesh. It is their dream that he should study well and qualify for medical college. Sunita puts in all her effort to motivate him. She repeatedly tells him that that is her life's ambition. Mohan provides all the financial help for extra coaching, and reminds Rajesh that all this is being done so that he will soon be a successful doctor. Rajesh is trying hard to fulfill his parent's dreams but the competition is so tough that he might or might not make it.

Situation 5: Bhasker drinks daily. He claims that he needs those two or three pegs to "unwind". His wife Jaya has noticed that over the years what was one peg occasionally has become three or more. She also noticed that her husband is querulous after drinks and she is unable to tackle his mood swings. Also, the situation is creating strain on their finances. Their frequent fights invite the curious looks of neighbours. Jaya most often gives in to crying fits and curses her fate.

None of these incidents are major disasters. They are all fairly common in the Indian milieu of life. They are also situations that we accept generally as fate and destiny. We think to ourselves that it happens to everyone, I need to work hard to succeed, and that there is nothing wrong in motivating your child to do well.

They result in the building up of stress, both mental and physical, in the minds and bodies of the concerned individuals. They are not able to, at this point of time, identify this as stress.

Getting back to Sarita's conflict with her in-laws regarding her sister-in-law Anita's visits, all of them have not yet realised that this has become a bone of contention for them. They are only looking at it as "a routine matter of conflict in most houses, something that will blow over with time, or something that people will get adjusted to." If they were aware of this as a *stressor*, they could iron out this problem with some dialogue, provided all concerned parties keep an open mind, and do not revert to stereotypes. By initiating a dialogue, all of them can get rid of the *stressor vis-a-vis* this issue and begin to enjoy their weekends. When smaller issues are resolved by dialogue, there will be an open door to discuss more serious matters like the issue of the house loan.

By neglecting issues, we are inadvertently causing a build up of stress. In this build up, every little thing counts.

I repeat, early intervention is the best remedy.

So, are we looking at a Utopian World where everything is perfect? Not really. We will continue to look at options to modify these situations and the other lifestyle changes as we go along.

Chapter 5
Coping with Stress

We have come to the point of identifying the presence of accepting that we are often stressed out to some

the search for remedies.

There are three golden rules:

One. It is very essential to know yourself.

Two. Early intervention is most effective.

Three. There is no single straight way of destressing yourself. Each one has to make his own choices from a multitude of options called coping skills. Each one must

want to adapt the one that suits them the best. Broadly, these techniques could be put under three headings:

    Task-oriented
    Emotion-oriented
    Distraction-oriented

When we say   , it means analysing the situation, the reasons for the way it went, and trying to

situation. Let us take the example of Ramesh who did not fare well in the examination. It would be rational for him to ask himself some questions to analyse the reason for the failure.

- Was his preparation adequate?
- If not, did he use short cuts like reading only anticipated questions, model papers, etc.?
- Did he honestly put in his best effort?
- Did he depend more on factors like luck and destiny than on actual preparation?
- Is he blaming someone else, like a teacher who did not tackle the subject adequately?

After introspection, he could get at some answers. Admittedly, this is not the easiest of exercises, and would require some maturity to arrive at solutions. But then, let us not equate maturity with chronological age; many youngsters are fully capable in analysing situations, given the opportunity. When one makes a habit of such analysis, it becomes an excellent safeguard against uncalled for *stressors*. It would well become a preventive tool, rather than a therapeutic procedure.

The second method is *emotion-oriented*. This involves dealing with one's feelings in a given situation. Once again I would like to go by the same example as before. Here the orientation would be to take a look at the person's emotions about the event, rather than at the problem. Some people are closely in touch with their feelings and easily express them. Others find it hard to express their feelings. Generally people who are aware of their feelings and who express them appropriately are emotionally healthy as compared to those who ignore them.

The first step in dealing with emotions is to recognise them when they occur. *An emotion is a felt tendency to move towards something as good or favourite, or to move away from something assessed as bad or unfavourable.* They are otherwise called "feelings".

- ❏ Is it fair to blame his parents for being unable to send him to medical college?
- ❏ Will it make him angry?
- ❏ Is it fair on his part to be belligerent with his sister because he feels his parents used their nest egg for her wedding? Will it make him feel frustrated?
- ❏ Is his insipient anger at his whole family justified?
- ❏ Is he feeling sad at his plight?

An important part of dealing with feelings is to accept them. People have a difficult time in accepting unpleasant feelings such as hurt and failure.

Feelings are like waves; if you ride them out, they will pass and leave you peaceful. If you fight them, they keep coming back.

The next step is to express them appropriately. That means doing something physical—speaking, writing, crying, shouting, or laughing. One may say that it is "acting out your emotions." Expressing feelings is sometimes best done physically, like shouting to yourself in a closed room when you are angry, or punching a pillow, or even banging a door or window, but doing nothing that will be harmful to others. For example, it is not okay to hit someone if you are angry. Once if one lets off steam by yelling to yourself or crying or by any other way, one can relax and calmly re-assess the situation that was triggered in the first place.

A simple way to practise this technique is to learn to verbalise your emotions. Ask yourself how many times in the past week you have said to yourself, or told a close friend your feelings. Some pointers:

- ➤ I'm angry
- ➤ I'm upset
- ➤ I'm hurt
- ➤ I'm sad
- ➤ I'm excited

- I'm anxious
- I'm frustrated
- I'm thrilled
- I'm nervous
- I'm lonely
- I'm stressed
- I'm touched

Try to be open about your feeling. Do not look at verbalising them as a sign of weakness in you. On the other hand, convert this line of thinking into a positive tool that will help you analyse and overcome *stressors*.

And then there are some societal stereotypes that are best avoided. *Boys and men do not cry.* I'm afraid I don't agree. Women in our society are allowed to cry. Some men carry this unhealthy message right through adulthood, and do not learn to express themselves emotionally.

It is acceptable to feel anything. Repressed emotions can accumulate and make it difficult for a person to function either emotionally or physically. Everyone needs to cry when that is what they are feeling. Your values are your rules for behaviour, more simply, what you view as right or wrong.

In our country, one could envisage the application of this method in dealing with the daily hassles of conflict between family members. Most of us are conditioned from childhood by certain unwritten and unspoken rules. That is, never to ask questions, never to verbalise your feelings, and to "accept" with a certain stoic sense of misplaced responsibility. And sometimes, it is given grandiose names like our culture, our tradition, *ad infinitum.* This is not to question the wisdom of the ages, but just to point out that times have changed, lifestyles have changed, and with the same enthusiasm with which we have accepted Internet and e-mail, we need to accept changing trends in interpersonal relationships, and its attendant obligations.

We will get back to Sarita and her mother-in-law's attitude differences towards the children. While each of them loves them in her own way, the grandmother is more indulgent with the children. Sometimes she lets other factors upset her like when her daughter Anita and Sarita have a difference of opinion. She is somewhat short-tempered with the children. On the other hand, Sarita is happy that she has loving in-laws to look after her children when they get back from school. When she is upset over financial commitments, she picks on her mother-in-law about little things like not attending to the kid's needs in time, etc.

We need to build and cultivate a strong support system; this may consist of family, friends, colleagues at work, etc. In the Indian milieu, the support system inherently exists, but instead of drawing from its strengths, we are letting ourselves be overwhelmed with the negative aspects of this system. Once again there are stereotypes: the elders know best, youngsters should not argue/talk and participate in discussions, obedience is the doctrine of Indian life, so on and so forth.

If we, in our closely-bonded families, could give dialogue and communication a chance, we would have been the most tranquil race; unfortunately, the opposite is true.

Let us go back to Sarita's family. Here are some questions Sarita might want to ask herself.

- Is it really so bad for a child to be pampered a bit?
- Can she not try to learn some skills of bringing up children from her mother-in-law?
- Are there some very obvious lapses in hygiene, medical matters that Sarita needs to take a firm stand on?
- Is she somewhat jealous that the pampering attitude of the grandparents might make the child lean more towards them?

- Is she letting other irritants influence her attitude?

Now here are some questions the mother-in-law, Kamala might want to ask herself.

- Is there some major flaw in what Sarita says?
- Is it hurting the child, or is it for the good of the child?
- Why should she not develop the attitude in line with the changed times?
- Sarita has the right to bring up her child in the way she feels best. Why should I impose what I feel is right?
- Shouldn't I be a loving grandparent and enjoy the child and help when asked to, rather than impose my views on how to raise the child?

These are some questions Vijay might want to ask himself.

- Since his father had discussed the commitment to the loan before taking it, and asked for some help, should he not contribute something towards the cause?
- Should he initiate a collective discussion about sharing weekends alternately at his sister's place and at his place, so that all of them feel relaxed?
- Must he not take a more active role in bringing up the children rather than leaving it all to Sarita?
- Should he not be demonstrative that he cares for his brother and parents by occasionally taking them out, or getting them small presents?

Let me reiterate that this is not a book of answers, but only one of helping you to literally hold a mirror to your psyche. Every single person must look to see what her/his particular situation is in relation to their lifestyle, and conduct a self-examination process. This is a very useful tool that requires repeated applications.

Remember, practise makes perfect!

The third tool is *distraction-oriented*. This probably is the easiest, and while it does not offer long-term solutions to *stressors*, it definitely helps in taking the edge away from them. Going for a walk, or a run, or washing the car, or digging and planting in the garden, even mundane activities like washing clothes come under this category. I must add that going out to meet friends, or seeing a movie also come under this category. Physical exercise literally distracts the mind's attention from the current *stressor*, plus gives an added benefit by releasing "feel good" hormones called endorphins, which help tremendously. In short, any physical activity that makes you sweat a little, does the trick. It instantaneously diverts the mind, and helps in getting back to a more rational situation from where you can look at the problem. While this does not resolve all conflicts, or chase away all the *stressors*, it may well give you the time to forget, and in many situations, that little time is sufficient for the situation to blow over.

You would have come to the conclusion that all or any one of them could help you in resolving issues.

However, mostly we do need some extra help in actually getting over the *stressors*. It is easy to say analyse your tasks or your emotions, but how to do this is the question.

It seems to be the time to take an inventory of emotional well-being before we proceed. Don't take your score too seriously; this is just for fun and whatever the score, it will only help you get better! Treat it as a starting point for an image overhaul.

There is a story of a person who would often say, "If a problem crops up today, I have no time till next fortnight to worry about it!"

Let us be amused with this person, smile a while, and try never to be like him.

1. I spend time doing work that I enjoy.
   a. Almost always
   b. Sometimes
   c. Almost never
2. I find it easy to relax.
   a. Almost always
   b. Sometimes
   c. Almost never
3. In my spare time I participate in activities that I enjoy.
   a. Almost always
   b. Sometimes
   c. Almost never
4. When I am about to be in a stressful situation, I realise it ahead of time and prepare for it.
   a. Almost always
   b. Sometimes
   c. Almost never
5. I handle anger:
   a. By expressing it in ways that hurt neither myself nor others.
   b. By bottling it up so that no one knows I am angry.
   c. By getting very aggressive.
6. I find it easy to express my feelings.
   a. Almost always
   b. Sometimes
   c. Almost never
7. I can talk to close friends, relatives, or others about personal matters.
   a. Almost always
   b. Sometimes

c. Almost never
8. When I need help with personal matters, I seek it out.
   a. Almost always
   b. Sometimes
   c. Almost never
9. When I am under stress, I make sure to exercise regularly to work out my tension.
   a. Almost always
   b. Sometimes
   c. Almost never
10. I participate in group activities like weddings; gatherings of relations, building/apartment functions, and office get-togethers.
    a. Quite often
    b. Once in a while
    c. Never

For each "a" that you have ticked off, give yourself 2 points.

For each "b" that you have ticked off, give yourself 1 point.

For each "c" that you have ticked off, give yourself a zero.

A score of 18 and more is Excellent

16 or 17 is Very good

14 or 15 is Good

And 13 or below means there is Scope for Improvement

Chapter 6
Recognising Stress

Now that you have arrived at your score, we will go through a long list of physical and psychological signs that will help you recognise your body and mind's reaction to any given *stressor*.

The trick is to monitor your body sensitively. Many people believe that they have to wait till they are suffering before they should take steps to reduce their stress.

That's not true. There is no reward for   and do not mistake it for fortitude. Fortitude is when you know how to monitor your body every step of the way. Watch for early signs.

it is true, the list is really long.

Physical signs

Pounding of the heart; heightened heart rate
Rapid, shallow breathing
Dryness of the throat and mouth
Raised body temperature
Decreased sexual appetite or activity
Feeling of light-headedness, dizziness or faintness

Tendency to be easily startled by small sounds
High pitched, nervous laughter
Stuttering and other speech abnormalities

- Difficulty in sleeping, or waking up in the middle of the night
- Grinding of teeth in sleep
- Restlessness—the inability to keep still
- Sweating, clammy hands, cold hands and feet
- Blushing
- The need to urinate frequently
- Diarrhoea, indigestion, upset stomach, nausea
- Migraine or other headaches
- Premenstrual tension or missed periods
- Body aches and pains, more than usual. Mainly, pain in the neck or lower neck
- Loss of appetite, weight loss; sometimes, excessive appetite, sudden weight gain
- Increased use of substances, in common language, tobacco, alcohol; sleeping pills, tranquilizers, drug addiction
- Accident proneness
- Frequent illness

That appeared like a list that can well cover every imaginable disease, but stress can do more harm to a person.

Also, there isn't a single symptom from which all of us have not suffered at different times in our lives.

Do not let the list intimidate you. This information may well help one to be alert. Forewarned is forearmed!

So look at it as a checklist, and when you are unduly feeling low, or have a nagging problem, just go through it to see if the problem is something that can be tackled by you, before you embark on runabouts of expensive tests and investigations.

Of course, if you are in doubt, consult your physician.

After that mind-boggling list of physical symptoms, we shall now look at some psychological signs that are giveaways that the person is under stress.

Remember, the idea is to monitor your body sensitively to stress.

Psychological signs
- Irritability, tension or depression
- Impulsive behaviour and emotional instability; the overpowering urge to cry or to run and hide
- Lowered self-esteem
- Thoughts related to failure
- Excessive worry, insecurity, concern about other people's opinion
- Reduced ability to communicate with others
- Increased awkwardness in social situations
- Excessive boredom
- Unexplained dissatisfaction with job or other normal situations
- Increased procrastination
- Feeling of isolation
- Avoidance of specific situations or activities
- Irrational fears
- Irrational thoughts
- Forgetting things more often than usual
- Missing planned events
- Guilt of neglecting family or friends
- Excessive work, omission of play
- Unresponsiveness and preoccupation
- Inability to organise oneself
- Getting overworked over small matters
- Inability to reach decisions, unpredictable decision making
- Inability to concentrate
- Feeling fatigued
- Loss of spontaneous joy

- Nightmares
- Mistrusting others
- Neurotic behaviour

This list is somewhat more difficult to identify except by the most astute individuals, and that too, only in the early stages. Obviously, in the later stages, one's judgment will be impaired.

A little earlier, we spoke of strong support systems—the family circle, friends or colleagues. It is for the close circle of family and friends to notice these little quirks in behaviour, and point it out to you, and for you to open up and discuss what is troubling you.

Here again, our so-called virtue of being strong and silent, of being tolerant and long suffering, our philosophy of just accepting it "as our fate", is probably not the best path to take. While it may not be wise to advertise your problems from the rooftop, a supportive family can be your jumping board, and the mentor to guide you on the road to recovery.

Having assessed your emotional well-being, it is now time to look at remedies.

I am not using the word "solutions", as we can only look at these as means for self-improvement.

How much benefit one derives from the various exercises, depends entirely on the person.

None of the exercises are difficult; it is but a matter of giving it your time and inclination.

Let me repeat, practise makes one perfect. For example, one would think that the simple act of breathing comes so naturally to us. It is synonymous with life itself. Still, all experts in stress management say that breathing exercises are some of the most effective destressing exercises.

Or to learn to play! We did it as children; we loved to play so much that we were upset when asked to stop our games. Today we are told that we need to go out and play to work out our tensions, to get those endorphins going, and to feel good.

It is like learning to put life into life by breathing easily and correctly.

To learn to be like the children we were, with a little time for everything.

Being aware that a problem exists is itself a victory; in the least, we can call it half a victory. When it comes to any one of the electrical implements in our house, we immediately look at the instruction manual when faced with a problem. When it is possible to identify the problem, the solution is simple. Most manuals give you instant remedies. It is only when one cannot put a finger on the problem that we read the ominous words, "please contact manufacturer."

In this case, the checklists help us identify the problem.

Chapter 7
Combatting Stress

With half the battle won, we will now move further

cannot but bestow victory on us. Like it is said in the

कर्मण्येवाधिकारस्ते मा फलेषु कदाचन ।
मा कर्मफलहेतुर्भूर्मा ते संगोऽस्त्वकर्मणि ।। 47 ।।

"To action alone hast thou a right and never at all to its fruit; let not the fruits of action be thy motive; neither let there be in thee any attachment to inaction."

Physical skills
Breathing exercises
Progressive relaxation
Stretching exercises
Walking
Sleeping

Mental skills
Meditating
Practicing yoga

Social skills
Meeting people
Keeping pets

Diversion skills
Activities that take your mind off the problem.

Spiritual skills
Introspection exercises to help you connect with yourself and nature to help you find a meaning to your life. Not to be confused or connected with religion.

Physical skills
These are things you can do for and with your body. This includes making sure that you take good care of your body. It helps in getting rid of stress. Physical relaxation techniques are useful in preventing stress and lowering your physical signs of stress. Try to set aside 20 minutes in your day to relax.

A. Breathing exercises
You can calm yourself by consciously controlling your breathing. Try one of these exercises:

Exhalation breathing: This slows your breathing to help calm you down.

1. Lie on your back with your arms at your sides.

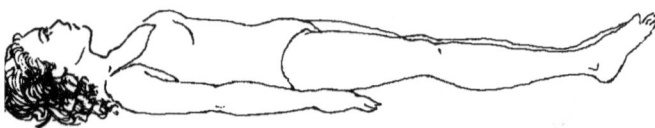

2. As you begin to breathe in, raise your arms towards the ceiling (elbows bent). Move your arms all the way up and over your head to the floor as you inhale.

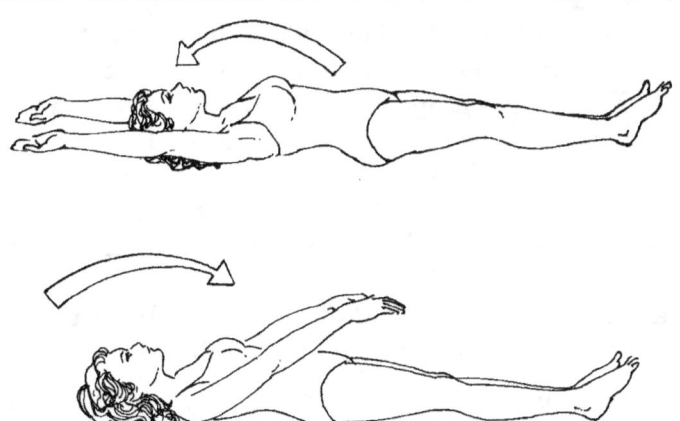

3. Reverse the order: breathe out (exhale) slowly and smoothly as you bring back your arms to your sides.

After you have done this several times, slowly inhale and exhale without moving your arms.

You can do this exercise for ten minutes or longer—it's up to you.

Deep breathing: It can be done anytime, anywhere. Deep breathing provides extra oxygen to the blood and causes the body to release endorphins, which are naturally–occurring hormones that re-energise and promote relaxation.

1. Slowly inhale through your nose, expanding your abdomen before allowing air to fill your lungs.
2. Reverse the process as you exhale.

Do this exercise for three to five minutes whenever you feel tense.

B. Progressive relaxation

This is a technique to help relax tense muscles.

1. Sit or lie down on your back in a comfortable, quiet room. Close your eyes.

2. Make tight fists, hold for five seconds, and then relax your hands. Do this three times. Pay attention to the different sensations of tension and relaxation. Concentrate on the sensations. If your mind tends to wander, and it will, get it back on line with positive effort.
3. Repeat step 2 with all of your muscle groups: arms, shoulders, chest, abdomen, back, hips, thighs, lower legs and feet.

At first, it may take about 20 minutes. With practise, you'll be able to do this in about five minutes.

Relaxation responses towards one's body during stress:

Stress response	Relaxation response
Rapid metabolism	Normal metabolism
Fast heartbeat	Normal heartbeat
Raised blood pressure	Normal blood pressure
Rapid respiration	Normal respiration
Tense muscles	Relaxed muscles
Blood supply to digestive system diverted	Normal circulation restored
Water retained in the body	Normal water balance restored
Immune resistance lowered	Immune resistance restored

And to think all you needed to do was relax! So, RELAX!

C. Stretching exercises

A stressed-out body causes all the muscles to be tensed, that is, muscles become hard and painful to touch.

If done correctly, stretching can promote relaxation and reduce stress. Have you ever noticed a cat stretch itself?

It is a slow and deliberate body stretch. Maybe it is time we learnt from cats!

Be very gentle and gradual in the stretching exercises. There should not be any abrupt or jerky movements, else you could injure your muscles. Do these exercises for five or ten minutes.

Stretch 1: Decide what muscles to stretch.

1. As you stretch, think about any one area being stretched; imagine the tension leaving as you gently take these areas to their comfortable limit.
2. Exhale into the stretch; inhale on the release. Breathe deeply and slowly—do not hold your breath.
3. Close your eyes for better awareness of your body's responses.

Stretch 2: Here's a stretch to relieve stiff muscles.

1. Sit up straight and inhale.
2. Exhale as you let your head move down to your chest. You'll feel a gentle stretch on the back of your neck and your shoulders.
3. Roll your right ear towards your right shoulder while inhaling. Drop your chin to your chest again while exhaling. Repeat to the left.
4. Drop your arms to your sides and push both shoulders forward. Slowly raise them towards your ears and circle them back and downward to the starting point. After two or three rotations, change directions.

There are other exotic methods for relaxing tense muscles. These include various forms of massage, relaxing baths in spas and aroma-therapy. While these are effective, I have chosen to explain two simple home remedies which are easy to practice and are easily available, also keeping the cost factor in mind.

D. Walking

Going for a walk can clear your mind, reduce tension and increase energy. Walking can help by providing a needed escape and it may increase the brain's production of endorphins (naturally occurring chemicals that relax and re-energise the body). If you step this up to jogging or running, all the better.

E. How to sleep better

If you can't sleep, then just get up. Don't even try to sleep. Just tossing and turning and watching the clock is not good for you. Here again, we need to break out of pre-conditioned stereotypes. It has since long been inculcated into our minds that the early hours of the day are the best for productive work, sleeping late into the morning is a social evil, so on and so forth.

Each person has for some strange reasons developed his own built-in clock. He has his own self-defined productive hours. His biorhythm dictates his waking and sleeping hours. So, instead of tossing and turning in bed at so-called specified sleep times, and making yourself more tense, get out of bed and into a comfortable chair. Read a book, watch television or play solitaire. Stay up as late as you like. Enjoy yourself.

Before you know it, you will be dozing. If you don't actually fall asleep, at least you will be relaxed.

The point is to reduce your anxiety about not sleeping and therefore make it easier to sleep.

Other tips:

Make an effort to:

- ❏ Resist the urge to nap during the day, no matter how tired you are.
- ❏ Don't exercise in the evening when you should be winding down.

- ❏ Avoid caffeine (coffee, tea, hot chocolate, or cola) after 2 p.m.
- ❏ Try drinking a mug of hot milk before going to bed.
- ❏ Consuming alcohol, as a treatment of sleeplessness, is best avoided.

A special word of caution. It has become more or less *de rigueur* to treat alcohol as the cure of all *stressors*. This is labelled as recreational drug use, and lately the phrase, "we work hard and play hard", is often heard. And to relax from the working hard mode and shift gears to play hard, we resort to substance abuse. It has been elevated to the exalted level of a cure-all for all *stressors*, and the ultimate manna to forget your troubles and sleep it all off in a blissful state, only to get up in the morning with a massive hangover that will impede your normal functioning, and possibly result in an increase in your tensions. Needless to say, in the long run, the detrimental effects of alcohol on your body are legendary. At the end of the day, you have not been able to identify your *stressors*, or try to look at alternatives.

Alcohol is not an alternative; neither is it a divertional tactic in resolving your *stressors*. Neither is alcohol a social skill, and the desire to "fit in" socially should not be the motivation for consumption.

It is addictive, and alters your thinking skills, giving you the so-called Dutch courage, and any decisions you may take under the influence, are highly unlikely to be rational.

Please ponder over this statement impartially. I am sure, a well-motivated individual like you will come to an identical conclusion.

While this book is not about drug abuse, considering the prevalence of the habit as a stress reliever, I take the liberty to explain the vicious cycle that fools and draws the newcomer into its net.

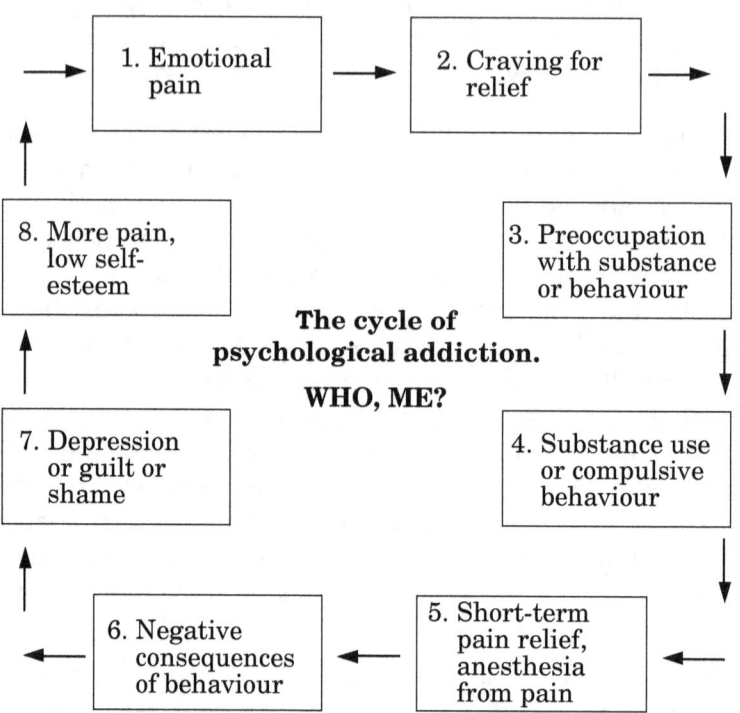

The cycle of psychological addiction.
WHO, ME?

Please respond true or false to the following statements to assess for yourself whether your perceptions correlate to scientific facts.

1. Alcohol kills brain cells.
2. Drinking alcohol can help a shy, inhibited person become outgoing, carefree and bold.
3. People who drink only beer or wine can never be problem drinkers.
4. People who drink only on social occasions are not problem drinkers.
5. Alcohol enhances sexual relations.
6. A person can die from drinking too much alcohol in one sitting.

The answers are as follows:

1. True.
2. False. Drinking is likely to make him foolish, giggly, and often delays the learning of social skills.
3. False. Depends on how much they drink, their reasons for drinking, and the consequences of their drinking behaviour.
4. False. Depends on all the factors given in question 3.
5. False. May provoke sexual desire, but hinders the performance.
6. True. So be careful how much you drink, especially if you have other medical problems.

You might think that a person once caught up in a problem would admit to it, and seek help to break out of it. In reality, it rarely happens so; if you state that an addiction problem has damaged his family, social and professional life, the chances are that he will reply with a "Who, me?" answer. "I'm having a little bit of a problem, nothing I cannot give up any time I want to!"

This "denial" often prevents the person concerned from seeking help. This book attempts to make people aware of their problems, identify them, and look for remedies.

When you know the enemy, half the battle is won.

The next step is to win the battle. Go for it!

Let us now relax, do a nice gentle stretch, and go to the next step.

Mental skills

These are things that you can do in your mind to help you cope with a situation. This makes your thoughts one of your most powerful coping skills.

A. Meditation

Meditation helps calm the mind so you can think calmly throughout the day. The goal is not for immediate relaxation but to increase serenity. Meditation puts you in control of your thoughts by forcing you to be present in the moment and to observe your thought processes. There is no point in starting to meditate unless you intend to make it a habit; you won't reap its benefits unless you practise on a regular basis. Also, it takes some time to learn this process. Do not lose heart if you cannot master it in a few sittings.

Fig. 1 : Meditation Posture

In the early stages, meditate for 10 to 15 minutes once or twice a day. Increase this to 20 minutes, not more than twice a day. Avoid meditating just before going to bed or you'll be too energised to sleep.

There are several meditation techniques. A simple method is explained below. One may however choose from a multitude of techniques available.

1. Choose a quiet room where you won't be interrupted.
2. Take time to relax; don't rush into it.
3. When you are thoroughly relaxed and breathing slowly and evenly, close your eyes. Slowly repeat a pleasant-sounding word over and over again in your mind as you breathe in and out. Continue in this state for 10–20 minutes.
4. To come back, begin saying your word out loud, deliberately and slowly. Pay attention to your breathing. Be aware of your body and your posture. Open your eyes and look around the room. After a minute or so, stand up and stretch.

With practise, you will eventually reach the point when you'll feel detached from your body and your physical surroundings while meditating. The world will fade from your awareness; you'll be in touch with your innermost self, deeply relaxed and thoroughly energised.

Note: Meditation can be overdone to the point where you are completely cut off from feelings of anxiety. This isn't healthy. Everyone needs a certain amount of stress in order to function.

B. Yoga

"Yoga," says Swami Abedadananda, in his book, *How to be a Yogi*, "is a Sanskrit word commonly used to signify the practical side of religion; and the first concern for the training for which it stands, to enforce proper obedience to the laws of our moral and physical nature upon which depend the attainments of perfect health and moral and spiritual perfection."

Patanjali's Yoga aphorisms are called the Indian practical psychology, as they not only enunciate the laws and principles of controlling the mind, but also teach how to translate them into action.

These are highly effective skills that are time-tested stress reducers apart from the sense of serenity they bestow on the individual—a literal awakening of the inner self. A part of our heritage, and India's gift to the rest of the world, these skills "are to be learnt from a well-versed guru/teacher, and not to be attempted from reading books." An initial introductory course should go a long way in helping a person de-stress.

So identify your teacher, and enroll for the preliminary session.

Yoga is identified as one of the best stress-busters. Again, practice makes perfect.

C. Transcendental meditation(TM)

A highly popular method for stress relief, TM, reduces the metabolic rate, lowers stress, and also lowers the concentration of various biochemicals in the blood which are associated with stress, such as cortisol. TM produces a state of rest, unique even to deep sleep or simple relaxation.

Again, this is a technique that has to be learnt from a teacher, and not from self-help books. While it requires only a few days to learn the basics, it will take more time to master the art and totally understand the concept. In the long run however, it is very beneficial.

As with most good things in life, do not expect immediate results; practised over a period of time, the results are very satisfying.

Social, diversional and spiritual skills

Social skills involve relationships. People and even pets are an important source of comfort; spend more time with them.

Relationships are like a delicate plant; they have to be nurtured carefully before they come to bloom.

Diversional skills are distractions. These don't require dealing with the problem directly; but are a way of taking your mind off what's happening. They are also the easiest way to de-stress in most circumstances.

Spiritual skills involve getting in touch with yourself to find meaning in your life. Tending to your spiritual life is an important way of dealing with stress, particularly if you experience a sense of loss in direction or meaning. Spirituality is not limited to religion.

Take some time to connect with yourself and with nature.

When it comes to social skills, we have a rich heritage of family and community. Inherently a society that comes together to celebrate or mourn innumerable occasions in life, either personal or community events like festivals, we can use it as a wonderful tool to build our support system. The sad part is, it is most often converted to an exercise where uncalled for comparisons leave a trail of negative emotions long after the event, making what should have been an enjoyable and supportive event into a literal pain that ought to have been avoided.

While the West is trying hard to reinforce the concept of family, let us not lose what has always been our heritage and strong point.

Spiritual skills

Many people equate spirituality with formal religion. While it is true that some find spirituality through formal religious practises, living by a set of rules is not what spirituality is all about. It is not measured by how often one goes to the temple/church/mosque/attends pooja and prayer meetings, etc.

Those who are satisfied with life regardless of their circumstances, are often spiritual. Their degree of satisfaction with life does not depend on their age, gender, life's circumstances, income or even health. Fulfilment of desires, be it of health or wealth, is not necessarily the highest standard of contentment. With deeper thought, it will bring in the realisation that it is but a path of further temptation.

Spirituality is tested in times of crisis. A spiritual person goes through trials with grace, peace and trust that whatever is happening, is happening for a good reason. Those without spirituality take hardships with bitterness.

My neighbour celebrated his hundredth birthday as per the Hindu lunar calendar. Shortly afterwards, he passed away peacefully in his sleep. To my knowledge, he was hardly ever sick, active till the end, and died in his sleep.

His wife, younger to him by about 10 years, accepted his death with the utmost tranquillity. For the better part of the day, that day, she sat on the swing where they always sat, and kept singing the *kirtans* he was so fond of hearing.

Some, including me, believed this to be her acceptance of the concept of the ultimate union of the soul with its maker. We were awestruck at the tremendous peace and tranquillity of this elderly lady.

Others said she had gone mad.

The lady went about her daily work as always, till it was time for her to leave this world.

Spirituality means a lot more than acceptance of death. In its very meaning, it encompasses the beautiful things in life.

Sometimes there is a tendency in India to treat spirituality as a routine or in the least, as a habit. I would suggest that one look at it as a joy—a happiness expressed in the fulfillment of the so-called habit. A happiness felt in the giving or the doing, without looking for rewards or pay offs that may accrue.

It is said that people have a hunger in their hearts, a vacuum that can only be filled with spirituality. A person who tries to fill this emptiness with possessions or worldly pleasures, stays empty.

Everyone at various times has questioned the very reason of his existence.

"Why am I here?", "What is the purpose of my existence",? "What purpose do I serve?"

Whenever people clear their mind of all other thoughts and look inside themselves to ask these questions, they are expressing a need for spiritual health.

It is the larger goal in life that people are in search of, the goal they look to whenever they experience the temporary futility in life's events, a goal to anchor their lives to.

Unfortunately, our society focuses more on the making of money than with connecting with oneself. This equates values with material possessions and is pleasure-centric.

It is time we decry the fact of this century and say,

"I am not for sale." And by corollary,

"Money cannot buy happiness."

There are no *quid pro quos* in life's transactions for spirituality.

Let us pause for a minute and see how we are faring on the spiritual equation, and see if we can quantify the pleasure you get from life.

Here is a scorecard to help you with this assessment.

When was the last time you:

1. shared ten minutes with a child and talked about a common interest?
2. went to a church, temple or any form of a religious place?
3. took a walk in the park or somewhere outdoors with someone you love?
4. watched the sun go down or come up, or searched for a rainbow, or enjoyed the drizzle of rain on your face?
5. spent half an hour listening carefully to someone different from you in age, culture, social class or simply, someone with totally different interests? Maybe your household help?
6. helped someone less fortunate than you? This need not be financial in nature.
7. read inspirational or devotional material? *Chicken Soup for the Soul*, or *Reader's Digest* will also come in this category.

8. spent 15 minutes pondering over or reflecting on your purpose of life?
9. prayed for the good of someone else?
10. attended an art exhibition, theatre or dance performance of a higher spirituality. I cannot classify popular cinema in this category.

Give yourself:
6 points for each activity that you did yesterday or today
5 points for each done in the last week
4 for each done in the last month
3 for each done in the last year

After totalling your score, some guidelines for interpreting the results are given below:

40-60   You are enjoying all the benefits of a spiritually-rich life.
30-39   You emphasize spiritual values in your life.
20-29   Spiritual concerns are a part of your life, but you may want to spend more time focusing on them.
0-19   Your spiritual side is underdeveloped. Maybe material aspects of life are taking up all your time and effort. Still, try to focus on a spiritual plane; you may well find the results beneficial.

Once we even mention the word "material" things of life, it literally opens up a Pandora's box of questions.

- How can I not expect to have the same comforts as the rest of my family or peer group?
- What is wrong in wanting to make your life more comfortable?
- How can I survive in the world without keeping up with the rest of the group?
- What will my children say if I do not give them the same sort of luxuries as their other friends have been getting. When they grow older, will they not chastise me for not leaving them enough property?

❑ If I do not stack up and store for the rainy day, what will happen to me?

Here are some suggestions to work yourself out of this maze:

❑ You are the best judge of what you want from life.
❑ You should not want to live your life to the expectations of others.
❑ Your very contentment should have a ripple effect, wanting others to emulate you.
❑ There is so much you can give your children besides wealth. You can make them happy, relatively tension-free individuals. They will be happier for it, and thank you, for while wealth may diminish with time, their happy attitude will only give them strength to brave the rough times with equanimity.
❑ And lastly, this little poem:

First I was dying to finish high school and start college,
And then I was dying to finish college and start working,
And then I was dying to marry and have children,
And then I was dying for my children to grow old enough for school,
And then I was dying to retire,
And now, I am dying,
And suddenly I realise,
I forgot to live!

Diversional skills

A physical activity is a good diversional skill. Apart from taking your mind off the current problem, it causes the release of endorphins, otherwise called the feel-good hormones, which in themselves pep up your mood.

By diverting your mind from the current *stressor,* it does not magically solve your problem, but it does give you valuable time to work off your initial resentment, anger or any other negative emotion. The endorphins released, induce a calming effect, and then, at the end of this diversional phase, if you still think you have a problem—most problems seem so insignificant after a little time—you are in a frame of mind to reason things out and take a positive step in resolving the issue.

The time-tested saying of counting to ten before you blast off is a mini-diversional skill.

A word of caution: Let us be clear as to what a physical activity is, and what a diversional skill is.

It must be remembered that any physical activity should be such that it does not cause harm to others or even you; not in the short-term, and not in the long-run.

Likewise, beating up someone, who is the target of your wrath or, in fact, anyone at all, is not a diversional skill. Essentially, it has to be harmless to one and all, and should have the capacity to expend some physical energy.

While punching a pillow when you are angry is okay, beating your wife or child, or anyone at all is not okay. Showing aggression on the ball with your bat is okay, wielding it as an instrument of terror to work off your frustrations is not okay.

Walking, jogging, running, games, etc., are excellent activities to work away your anger and problems.

All these physical activities stimulate the brain in producing endorphins—the pleasure-producing hormones, otherwise popularly called the feel-good hormones. They are continuously produced in response to healthy activities, and many times, the brain continues to produce them even after the conclusion of the activity.

Training for some useful physical activity is a good idea; as it will make you automatically gravitate to it when you feel the need of a physical activity.

So, besides maintaining a regular regimen of physical activity, using the same to de-stress gives you double benefit by keeping your endorphins flowing.

Having said all this, we will now come to the most important point of all questions.

Where is the time for all this?

Chapter 8
Finding the Time

Where is the time for all this?
This question functions as a two-pronged   In the primary sense, bad organisation of time is in itself a major

And, in the secondary sense, using the lack of time as a reason for introspection and revaluing priorities compounds the problem which takes us on to the topic of time management.

A zest for living

> "If you want to enjoy the greatest luxuries in life, the luxury of having enough time, time to rest, time to think things through, time to get things done and know you have done them to the best of your ability, remember there is only one way. Take enough time to think and plan things in the order of their importance. Your life will take a new zest, you will add years to your life, and more life to your years. Let all things have their place and let each part of your business have its time."
> —Benjamin Franklin

After all, a day has 24 hours, and there are just those

do not waste it. Not really; you can make money but you cannot make time.

us try to save our money and invest it wisely, how much more should we try to avoid wasting our time and invest it with energy to good effect?

- ➤ Yesterday is a cancelled cheque.
- ➤ Tomorrow is a promissory note.
- ➤ Today is ready cash. Use it.

Here are some simple pointers to help you make the best use of your time:

Prioritize your activities: Sounds simple, but isn't. If you get through this one, you've won more than half the battle. Sometimes, and many times, we are so absorbed in pursuing our goals that we feel there is no time for anything else. Let me tell you about an incident.

In a rural area of America, a farmer and his dog would sit on the fence watching trucks go by on the highway. Whenever a truck went by, the dog would chase after it till it was out of sight.

One day, the farmer's friend said, "Do you think your dog will ever catch a truck?"

The farmer replied, "That's not what worries me. What worries me is what he would do with it if he caught one!"

Many of us in life are like that little dog. We give our lives pursuing goals that have little value even if we reach them. Sometimes, it pays to stop and ask whether we have objectives worth pursuing.

Plan your schedule in brackets of an hour : Nothing is too simple or silly to go into this category. If it is important to you, mark it out. Don't forget sleep time.

When you are setting up a sort of timetable like you used to have in school, give particular attention to what you want to do, however simple or insignificant it may seem to be. Remember in school you had more maths classes than say social studies. Just goes to reinforce the concept of prioritising.

Keep time logs till you get used to the idea : Doing it always is, of course, excellent. Inasmuch as we may want to think that we can retain everything by rote, putting things down on paper is good. The organisers available in the market generally have time bars marked out in spaces of two hours. It is a great help in demarcating your day. This is not only for busy executives; everyone, from the school kid to a housewife, needs it.

Do not procrastinate: Never put off for tomorrow what you planned to finish today. The word procrastinate is the number one time waster. You can call it the thief of time. Be tough with yourself, and banish this trait from your life. Start off by doing something that you have been putting off, a difficult task you must tackle, an apology long overdue, money you owed someone, whatever.

> He slept beneath the moon,
> He basked beneath the sun,
> He lived a life of going-to-do,
> And died with nothing done.

Delegate: Don't try to run the whole show yourself. Many of us like to believe that most tasks are best done by ourselves, that depending on others is often risky. Here, good leadership counts. That is, to have a good assessment of who is best capable of that job. Obviously, in an office or a home, one person simply cannot do everything. Delegation is a must.

Identify the correct person and instruct him in easily understandable terms. For example, do not just say to a child, "go and buy bread", but explicitly tell which shop to go to, which brand to buy, and how much it is likely to cost.

The most important thing is to "ask", and not order. Delegation does not mean ordering a person to do something. It means identifying and matching the person and the task and then making the person feel important that he is being identified for the task.

Take on tasks within your limits: Learn the difference between aggressive and assertive behaviour. In short, learn the art of saying "NO" when you must.

Here, one needs to differentiate between assertive action and affirmative action. Let us look at a situation where people are standing in a queue for railway tickets. Someone simply pushes ahead of you and tries to get to the window faster. One usually grumbles about people who do not behave, etc. This is *non-assertive behaviour*. Telling the person that you are ahead of him, and that he should get to the rear of the line, is *affirmative behaviour*.

To form happy relationships, one must express wants and needs in a way that is respectful to others. To find the happy compromise between timidity and assault is to be assertive, rather than aggressive. To be assertive, one needs to be upfront in saying what you mean, and not tiptoeing around dropping hints. This does not come naturally to a lot of us, and has to be consciously practised.

Particularly, we as a race are conditioned to tiptoe around issues, and expect the other party to understand our predicament. And then we are quick to take umbrage at the non-compliance of the other party!

All this in the name of our heritage. In these times, this very same trait is harming our health, and we must look into the applicability of this trait in today's situations.

I am sure you will agree with me that we have to learn to say what we mean, and more specifically, learn to say NO when we mean NO.

Telephone eats up time: Make calls during specific time periods. This goes for receiving calls too. Ditto for unexpected visitors. Unexpected calls at the wrong time can wreck your schedule, as will unexpected visitors. While it is commonplace to make an appointment to see the doctor or meet an important person, it is generally believed that good friends and relatives can be imposed upon. It would be a good idea to cultivate the habit of checking with the person whether he/she is free to have a long talk with you at that point in time. An honest "no" should not affront you or make you think negatively about the concerned person. What generally happens is that the person who has said that he is busy just now, "is too big for his boots", "forgot how much you did for him when he needed your help", etc. It is time that we took the statement for what it is, and set up a convenient time for a long dialogue.

The same goes for unexpected guests. While they should be made welcome, it is not fair that you are expected to manipulate your time schedules to suit their pattern. The status of a guest in our heritage—he is equal to God. Let's say that in today's world, the way things are going, even the good God may have to take an appointment to meet you! Jokes aside, prior intimation before dropping by, and adjusting to the host's lifestyle and time schedules would be a good practise. And like they say—

> *Some make you happy when they come;*
> *Some make you happy when they go!*

Keep some personal time at the end of a day: Use this to review your time utilisation. More so in the case of busy mothers who are so carried away with their duties, that they deprive themselves of this personal time. Believe me, the 15 minutes spent on yourself will recharge your energies spectacularly, and endow you with a sense of serenity that you will cherish, besides helping you cope with your responsibilities better.

Remember, there is a lot of substance in what was said eons ago that holds good even today.

There are two days in a week that should be totally stress free. One is yesterday, because it is of no consequence now, and the other is tomorrow, as it is yet to happen.

> Salutation to the Dawn
> Look to this day!
> For it is life, the very life of life.
> In its brief course
> Lie all the varities and realities of your existence:
> The bliss of growth
> The glory of action
> The splendour of beauty
> For yesterday is but a dream
> And tomorrow is only a vision
> But today well-lived makes every yesterday
> A dream of happiness
> And every tomorrow a vision of hope
> Look well, therefore, to this day!
> Such is the salutation to the dawn.
> —Kalidasa

Chapter 9
Stress and Children

It hurts me to write this chapter, as I am sure it will disturb you to read it. I have campaigned fervently for all of us to be knowledgeable, to be aware of troublesome situations and to use all the tools available to us in

anxiety does not attack; it is only we who choose to think that way.

But when the parents possess anxiety while bringing their children to doctor's clinics with the complaint of certain problems, I believe it is time to look at this problem from every conceivable angle, and to try everything in our means to stem this rot.

Some years ago, it was inconceivable that a child be labelled "stressed". "How can a child be stressed?" would have been the question. Today, in our modern world, things being what they are, young babies are left in the care of strangers, be it household help or crèches run mostly by untrained hands. Every psychologist will tell

is likely to encounter in a normal household. Normally, a couple of decades ago, this would have been done when

Pre-nursery school admissions begin when the child is two-and-a-half years old. We are not attempting to look at dysfunctional families, just normal life situations that can be *stressors* for little children.

Stress and Children

The fact is that it is difficult to provide readymade answers to such problems. Each couple must arrive at their own choice. The only redeeming factor is that this is not the only cause for anxiety. As the children grow, unfortunately, the parents add considerably to their stress.

Another cause is the arrival of a sibling in the family. The child may feel "threatened" that the new arrival is a competitor and would share the affection of the parents. Intelligent parents can handle this easily, and most often the child learns to accept the new baby.

As the years go by, coping with the syllabus, and competitiveness add to stress. To this add interpersonal problems like quarrels with the "best friend", jealousy, possessiveness with toys, etc. All these seem very trivial and most adults don't take particular notice of them, but they are of paramount importance to the child. Parents must make time to listen to the problems of the child and not arbitrarily dismiss them as "rubbish".

Let us go back to Surendranath's family and see if we can see some trouble spots there. Sarita and Vijay have two children, Pooja and Raju. While Sarita works, the grandparents look after the children. Sometimes there is a conflict about the needs of the children, and sometimes extraneous matters that are troubling the parents are the cause of conflict between the grandparents and parents. In short, the children are made pawns in a game of conflicting egos.

Pooja asks her grandmother to pack her something more exciting than the usual breakfast as all her classmates get exotic pizza and noodles. The grandmother can agree to learn to cook these new dishes and promise that in a few days she will oblige. Sarita can step in and make her kids favourite dishes once in a while, or criticise her mother-in-law for not obliging her kids. This can go on and on.

In this simple example, we can see the right and wrong signals the elders can pass on to their children and sow seeds of further behavioural patterns.

Most often, the unfulfilled desires of the parents are the pressure points in a child's life. The parents unconsciously or sometimes consciously put pressure on the child, especially in the month of May–June, when they seem to be largely stressed-out and anxious. It is a time for happiness for some, recriminations for others and sorrow for a few.

The sad part is the number of suicides at this time of the year because of failure in examinations.

- Who has made the child so conscious of failure?
- Who failed to prepare him for alternatives?
- Who has set standards that were obviously unattainable by the student?
- Who has not instilled in him enough self-esteem that he can take failure in his stride, and use it as a stepping-stone to other achievements?
- Who has made him feel so unworthy that he is unable to face his family and is fed up with life?

While every human being has a right to lead his life as he chooses to, I believe none of us have the right to distort or mutilate the lives of another individual, especially when that individual is handicapped by virtue of age to realise what is being done to him, or for the same reason, incapable of retaliating.

The following lines of Kahlil Gibran illustrate best the relationship between a child and a parent. The emphasis is on the strengths of the parent in moulding his ward's energies, always accepting him as an individual in his own right, and not a carbon copy of himself.

> *Your children are not your children.*
> *They are the sons and daughters of*
> *Life's longing for itself.*
> *They come through you but not from you,*
> *And though they are with you yet*
> *   they belong not to you*
> *You may give them your love*
> *   but not your thoughts,*
> *For they have their own thoughts.*
> *You may house their bodies but not their souls,*
> *For their souls dwell in the house of tomorrow, which*
> *   you cannot visit, not even in your dreams.*
> *You may strive to be like them, but*
> *   seek not to make them like you.*
> *For Life goes not backward*
> *   nor tarries with yesterday.*
> *You are the bows from which your children*
> *   as living arrows are sent forth*
> *The archer sees the mark upon the path*
> *   of the infinite, and he bends you with His might*
> *that His arrows may go swift and far.*
> *Let your bendings in the Archer's*
> *   hand be for gladness:*
> *For even as He loves the arrow that flies,*
> *   so he loves also the bow that is stable.*

What do we really want for our children?

All children come into this world with the potential for reasonable success. It is just that sometimes we do not take care to give them the right guidance. One cannot buy an annual guidance contract from a company and leave all the problems to them.

Our children are being raised in an atmosphere of anxiety that is automatically carried on to them. We often ingrain into their young minds statements like, "It is time for you to worry about your exams."

Unfortunately, most children are being raised in an atmosphere of lopsided priorities. They are raised in an atmosphere of intense competitiveness, raised with a belief that to fail to achieve is a mortal sin.

We are breeding future generations of anxiety prone individuals, and make them suffer from heart attacks and other ailments etc.

"I will do for my children what my parents have done for me," is the prevalent attitude. It is possible that it is this inconstancy in behaviour that confuses the child and breeds stress.

And to repeat an often heard line, early intervention is the best. In the case of children, adult patterns must be modified when the child is in the womb! The world is perfect; there is no anxiety in it anywhere.

Let us look at some of the causes and effects of stress in some detail.

Intense striving and competitiveness
Many decades earlier, in a PTA meeting, I witnessed a very upset mother who was questioning the teacher as to why and how her daughter got less marks in the examination when compared to the previous examination. She blamed the teacher of inefficient monitoring of the child's work, and punished her daughter heavily for poor performance by banning her from playtime till she did better. She herself was extremely upset. The child was only 5-year-old.

Extreme organisation and achievement
Today's child is expected to come first in class, be a proficient and highly talented tennis player/Bharatanatyam dancer, learn some extra skills and extra language or computer,

and even be good in traditional recreational activities like swimming or playing a game, etc. From waking up time to bedtime, each hour is structured. There is no free time, here free time being time to play or time to relax—even playtime is structured. Interacting with other children is virtually absent.

All that not only stresses the child but the parent too. I am sure all this is happening because we are letting it happen. If someone else's child is able to do this and more, then why not mine?

I am sure most of the parents are doing this. They believe that it will help the child cope with the world, but they must remember, "Life is what is happening to us as we are busy planning other things." I am sure we are not conscious of some of our actions that are leading to this stressfull pattern of life.

I will attempt to enumerate some of the more common interactions between adults and children that *encourage children to choose anxiety as a lifestyle.* Then you can look into the applicability *vis-a-vis* specific situations. Remedial action would then be simple.

1. *Pressure-filled, non-relaxing kind of life.* Hurrying through everything and expecting the child to talk early, to get toilet training early, even before their young bodies are capable of coordinating such mind–body responses, to learn the alphabet early, recite rhymes early. It is generally pushing to accelerate the normal developmental pattern that is unique to each child. One will notice that these days schools have a pre-nursery class, which admits children at the age of two-and-a-half or three. There are crèches where the little infant is taught discipline, and alphabets and numbers. All with the approval of the parent.
2. *Putting all the emphasis on being better, faster*

and smarter than others. In this pursuit, the achievements that are not visible to the world are neglected; for example, inner growth, where the child nurtures small skills like being helpful to others, contemplative attitudes like realising what exactly he wants from life translated into a child's vocabulary, the things he would like to do, to communicate with parents about things other than school achievements, to develop good peer bonding and so on. It appears what is important are those skills that can be displayed to the world, like brilliant report cards, trophies, awards, etc. While all competitiveness is not bad, and encouraging the child to do well is not bad, a middle path should be the best.

3. *Comparing one's children with other children, especially the siblings.* There are sayings in practically all Indian languages that all fingers of the hand are not equal. Grandma's wisdom is unparalleled, but while we choose to quote it when it suits us, comparisons with friends and relatives' children is a very common practise. On the flip side, if a child said to you that so and so's father has this much wealth or this position, and why are you lacking behind, how would you react?

"Behave yourself, and stop talking back to parents!"

Or a recitation of the litany of mishaps that prevented you from reaching that exalted position.

When you blame the child, you are sowing the seeds for this sort of passive aggression, or putting the blame of his actions on other events/situations/people.

4. *Referring to a child's past mistakes.* While a child may have committed a mistake like breaking a

tumbler, repeatedly telling him that he cannot be trusted to carry water in a tumbler because he broke one, will only reinforce a negative trait.

To help them learn from their mistakes, focus on their achievements rather than their shortcomings.

5. *Using guilt or threats.* Saying things like "Wait till your father comes home" or "You should be ashamed of yourself" or "How could you do this after all I have done for you", should be avoided. These are actions that subtract from a child's self-worth and make him dislike himself. Occasionally, it may also provoke aggressive behaviour which might be visible later in life towards society at large and sometimes, at the perceived perpetrators of this psychological insult.

6. *Refusing to allow children to grow independently* by advising them at all steps, refusing to allow them to make any decisions, or chiding away any that they have made as foolish and without merit. Citing age as a right to claim to be well-informed is the prevalent tendency. Telling them how much they owe you and how much you did for them and that they should be ashamed to leave home and live separately just as you are growing old and need them, are all fostering dependency rather than independence.

7. *Teaching them to worry.* Statements like, "Examinations are only a few weeks away, and you better start worrying about them", cause stress in children.

8. *Punishing children without explaining* why they are being punished and not making them understand what was wrong. "I did what I was told, and no one explained anything to me!" is the common answer. Making a child suffer insult without explaining to him the cause and also the consequences of his bad behaviour will not serve any purpose other

than the child harbouring some resentment. Try explaining patiently, and without anger, and you will find the exercise well worth the effort. Also, correcting/punishing children in front of others needs to be avoided.

9. *Complaining about life in front of children.* Complaining about relatives, colleagues, bosses and making disparaging remarks about them that inculcates in a child only contempt and intolerance towards others. Discussing business deals and some sharp practises involved in front of children or making them feel that a little bit of dishonesty is absolutely okay, or the attitude that money can buy one out of most situations and also buy a person whatever he wants even though he is incapable of earning the same with his own skills and merits, is a very counter-productive attitude.

10. *Not talking to them about their own lives, concerns, fears and personal issues.* Being their judge, critic, warden rather than friend, confidante and advisor, all lead to stress.

Today, child specialists and psychologists are treating children as young as three-years-old for stress-related symptoms. How does one identify the child who has a problem?

1. Temper tantrums like breaking things and pulling hair.
2. Refusing to eat.
3. Aggressive behaviour with other children and siblings.
4. Withdrawing into himself and not mixing with other children.
5. Robbing and telling lies.
6. Stammering and bed wetting, and grinding of teeth while asleep.

7. Inattentiveness in school and complaints from the teacher that his behaviour and attentiveness has altered.
8. Demanding behaviour, and insisting that his demands be fulfilled instantly.
9. Inflicting injury on his person to draw attention, or crying till he is virtually breathless.
10. Truant behaviour the child leaves home for school, but does not go to school and returns home at the appropriate time as if he has just returned from school.

If a parent notices any of these traits over a period of time, seeking professional help is the best remedy. Try to avoid justification of these traits with aphorisms like "he is only a young kid", "they say his father/mother used to behave just like this", and so on.

The toys we buy for children to keep them amused can play a vital role in shaping their minds. While nurturing toys like cuddly ones make for more security and encourage a loving nature, aggressive toys like guns and other weaponry, and fast toys like cars and other racing vehicles, breed a tendency towards aggression, and a habit of speed; of getting there fast, no matter how! Do we see the seeds of road rage here?

How inadvertently we influence a child's psyche!

"Dolls are for girls as cars and guns are for boys," is a rapidly changing trend all over the world. Such gender labelling is unwanted, and nurturing soft toys have become universally popular. Similarly, children love instructive and educative toys. They teach as well as entertain.

Buying is no longer a simple matter where the price dictates issues; it needs to be looked into as a tool to help a child grow in the right direction.

As adults, it is time we grew out of our ingrained prejudices, and stop quoting the old encompassing excuse, "In my childhood, I did what my father said," and attempt to look ahead. It is a rapidly changing world, and with the same astuteness that we accepted and got used to certain conveniences, we should also attempt to learn more about child psychology so that we can help our children get used to this rapidly changing world. And to take care of their mental health with the same cautiousness with which we meticulously attend to their vaccination schedule.

> When I was a child, I spoke as a child, I understood as a child, I thought as a child; but when I became a man, I put away childish things.
>
> —Corinthians XIII.II

Train a child in a way he desires to grow. When he is old, he will not depart from it.

Here is a description of the "modern" youth.

"Our youth loves luxury. They have bad manners, contempt for authority; they show disrespect for their elders, and love to chatter instead of exercise. Children are now tyrants, not the servants of their households. They no longer get up when their elders enter the room. They contradict their parents, chatter before company, gobble up their food, and tyrannise their teachers". And this has been said centuries back by Socrates.

Just goes to show that the elders had the same sort of perceptions about youth from way back in the past, or that the youth have always had it in them to march to their own drums, away from the beaten path. All that has been said in this chapter reinforces the idea that it is the elders in the first place who have installed certain preconceived notions in children during the formative years; and when the added pressures from sources external to the family result in a period of probable readjustment or even sometimes maladjustment, it has been labelled rebellion!

Most of the time, I lay the blame squarely on the parent. In a rapidly changing world where adapting fast is the watchword, they must give the youngsters some breathing space. They have their own problems apart from those that are common to most of us. The biggest of them is to find a satisfying career, to live up to their parents' expectations, sometimes prove themselves in fields totally contrary to their own dreams, smaller things like keeping up with today's trends, be it in clothes, coffee bars, bowling alleys or water sports. Come to the parents—think this over. Did you have to cope with such situations? Did these things even exist over the horizon for us? Didn't we live in a simpler and far less competitive world?

It is a rapidly changing world; give the kids a little time to adapt; to make their choices, to follow their dreams. And no. The parent is not always correct; he is not the fountainhead of all knowledge, and difficult as it is to accept, every parent has made his/her own share of mistakes, blunders, wrong decisions, "Ah, yes, that is why I want to protect my child from all the mistakes I did!" You must realise his life is different from yours. The times are different, and the choices are different! And more importantly, he has to make his own mistakes and learn from them.

I genuinely believe that children have an immense potential to make the world a happier place for themselves and everyone else. So, my young friends, here is some advice:

There are seven major crimes:
- I don't think
- I don't know
- I don't care
- I am too busy

- I live well enough alone
- I have no time to read or find out
- I am not interested

Remove the negative ideas from each of these markers, and you will have a beautiful world open up before you.

Up to a point, a man's life is shaped by environment, heredity and movements and changes in the world about him. Then there comes a time when it lies within his grasp to shape the clay of his life into the sort of thing he wishes it to be. Only the weak blame parents, their race, their times, lack of good fortune, or the quirks of fate. Everyone has it within their power to say, "This I am today; that I will be tomorrow."

Chapter 10
Stress and Indian Women

It is a given fact that stress as well as all the tools to combat it are common to everyone. In our country, women are often the target of innumerable social injustices and blind prejudices.

Indian woman are one subjected to special conditioning a special teaching from the cradle upward that makes her accept many prejudices as a part of life, as a part of destiny, as something that happens to every woman, and that she is the rule and can never hope to be the exception. While it is impossible to enumerate and list the various prejudices, they are of interest in that these ingrained notions add tremendously to the stress levels of women. Many times, the lady is not even aware that she has a problem and is again conditioned to accept it as a part of her life. She is called upon frequently to fall back on her so-called tremendous resources of will power.

ranath's family. There are four ladies in the house:

> Kamala, the eldest lady of the house, wife, mother, mother-in-law, and grandmother.
> Sarita, who is about thirty-year-old, is the daughter-in-law of the house, and the wife of the eldest son. She is a working woman, educated to college level, and mother of two school-going children.
> Anita, the daughter of the house, twenty-four-year old, educated to college level and recently married. She lives in the same town as her parents.

❑ Pooja, a seven-year-old girl, is the granddaughter of the house, daughter of Sarita; she studies in an English-medium school along with her younger brother, five-year-old Raju.

This is an urban family, where all the members are educated, and where all of them get along reasonably well. Yet there are some stereotypes that they are unable to avoid.

Kamala

Kamala is an understanding mother-in-law, and concurs with Sarita's need to work. She looks upon her job as an additional source of income for the family, and does not mind the "privileges" she is losing out on because Sarita is a working woman. She also does not mind looking after the grandchildren. However, there are times when she is upset.

Sarita keeps back part of her salary in her personal account. After all, is it not her duty to hand-over all her earnings and then be given some money to spend.

Does Sarita need all those clothes? Do the children need to be dressed in the latest fashions?

Is Sarita saving enough for little Pooja's dowry? As it is, Pooja does not have a fair complexion, and therefore, more dowry may be demanded.

Anita is newly wed, but already nearly a year has passed. Why is she not pregnant?

Anita is, after all, the daughter of the house; why does Sarita get upset when she comes every Sunday?

Anita must learn to adjust more in her married home. She seems to be in conflict with her husband sometimes about various things. Even though she is educated, she must learn to hold her tongue.

She would love to die before her husband, but who will look after him if she predeceases him? At least they have the house as some sort of security for their old age, but there is the loan, and Vijay helps occasionally. If only Sarita could help! And who will look after her if she outlives her husband?

All these issues constantly come to her mind. They give her headaches and hypertension. Some of them she cannot ignore, and some she can discuss with others.

Kamala's concerns are a part of her upbringing. They are part of a mindset created during her childhood; and while she has admirably adjusted to changing norms, some prejudices that are harmful in the long run, remain.

Her preoccupation with Pooja's complexion and the thought of her dowry will sow the seeds of insecurity in Pooja, and make her lose her self-esteem. If ever she faces some rejection from a potential marriage alliance, she may consider herself a burden on the family.

Also, her preoccupation with Anita not starting her family, her constant questioning the same, her interference in matters concerning husband and wife, are all traditional mindsets that centuries of education have been unable to undo. She will continue to believe that daughters must tow the line in the in-laws house. After all, not all can be as lucky as Sarita to have an understanding mother-in-law like her. Come what may, she must acquiesce.

These are additional *stressors* in a woman's life that take away from her peace of mind. On the flip side, religion is a big solace, but sadly there are times when ritual takes the place of religion, adding to financial problems.

Sarita
Sarita is happily married, has an income of her own that she partly saves for herself, and has two children.

She is aware that her in-laws' presence is a stabilising factor in her children's life. The grandparents dote on them and are more than indulgent. Why then is she taciturn over small things her mother-in-law suggests? Is it because that she is conditioned to believe that both she and her in-laws are at different poles, and an amicable relationship is really not possible?

The same goes for Anita's visits. As a person who has known her from the time she was a teenager, she could easily talk it over with her, or simply ask her to help out in the kitchen so that the work is shared. Is it an in-built prejudice that is holding her back?

Does she need to complain to her husband about all trivial matters that she can well sort out? Or is she unwittingly falling into the trap of having him take sides? Did she at any time reassure her in-laws that they are very much needed and loved members of the family, no matter what the circumstances are?

Indian women do not give or ask for such reassurances. Everything is implied; everything is taken for granted; everything is a "duty", however unpleasant it may be. And if the fulfilment of the duty makes both parties extremely unhappy, it is fate and to be borne stoically with a lot of verbal bickering, but never to be discussed, never to have a dialogue and never to search for other alternatives that are acceptable to both parties.

Is she going to sit down with her daughter and reassure her that beauty is but skin deep, and that all of them love her unconditionally? Will she encourage her to study well and emphasize the importance of a career? Or will she give in to the traditional mindset that colour and complexion are important. Are those born without beauty a burden in the marriage market?

Will she teach her son that all the work in the house is

not the responsibility of the lady, and that he should also begin to share the housework as he grows older? Will she educate her mother-in-law and others in the house that in these times there are no gender-based roles, and it is essential that all children learn all skills? Or will she, in spite of being at the suffering end of balancing a career and home, still insist that it is a male prerogative to sit and order the women in the house?

Will she teach herself and discuss with her husband that in these times children are likely to leave the house to make a career for themselves, that they may marry outside their caste or even religion, and they should prepare themselves to accept such situations as and when they happen?

Will she give her children the freedom to make choices, and to grow at a pace that they decide? Or will she insist that it is the duty of her children to stay with them and look after them in their old age?

Sarita seems to be the sort of a person who will identify *stressors* as and when they happen with an open mind. She is likely to diffuse the situation with a lot of adaptability.

Anita

Will Anita allow her mother to interfere in her own and her husbands' decision about starting her family because it is the norm in most Indian households?

Will she assert herself if her in-laws don't treat her fairly? Or will she succumb to the theory that come what may, she has to accept whatever is meted out to her in her marital house?

If required, will her parents and brothers stand by her, and not say that her place is in her in-laws' house, and once married away, that she has no place in her parents' house?

Will she adjust with her sister-in-law, Sarita, who was her friend and confidante till she got married, or will she let age-old prejudices hurt a friendly relationship?

Pooja

Will Pooja grow up free from the shackles of years old mindsets to emerge as a capable, strong young lady who has the courage to take decisions, however hard they might be?

All this reads like a great Indian saga, but where is the stress in all this, you might want to ask.

Right in the beginning we discussed that *stressors* come in two forms, major life issues and daily hassles.

Most women have to bear with more than their fair share of hassles than the average man. And like we repeatedly agreed, stress has the capacity to add up, and when this heavy load adds up, it tells on the health of the woman.

As women are better empowered, the pulls of tradition and rational thinking are at present further adding to their stress levels. Women are in a stage of transition, and this phase is likely to be harder than simply treading on the beaten path.

General practitioners, gynaecologists and psychiatrists will vouch for the fact that women are more prone to stress-related disorders than their male counterparts.

The common symptoms are:

- Fatigue
- Backache
- Headache
- Indigestion and problems of the digestive system
- Disinclination toward sexual activity
- Chest pain
- Various menstrual problems
- Infertility

- Eating disorders like comfort gorging or anorexia
- Anxiety disorders that include palpitations
- Depression
- Hysterical attacks
- Suicide

The various stresses in a woman's life present themselves as vague aches and pains for which a definitive clinical entity cannot be identified. Perforce, they have to be labelled as the consequences of stress.

Depression is a major problem in almost all women above the age of sixty. These woman "will" themselves to remain somewhat melancholic as they believe that pleasure and laughter at their age is passè, or that to say that they are happy will bring down the evil eye on them; it is safer to say that things are just about bearable, rather than say, they are pretty much on even keel.

Is there no getting away from all these hassles that are eventually making you ill?

The answer is once again in awareness.

Awareness that many things are trivial.

Awareness that in case of major issues one should not let age-old prejudices come in the way of rational thinking; that communication and dialogue would help in reaching better options.

Awareness that there are options for all things, if only we look for them.

Awareness that being born as a woman does not mean that you are a second-class citizen.

Awareness that you have the right to good health as much as anyone else, and that you will exercise that right by making the correct choices.

Some suggestions

- ❑ Take good care of your diet. Feeding others does not look after your health.
- ❑ Exercise for a little time daily, and practise a skill like yoga for a few minutes. Where is the time with all the things that are happening? You can make time if you will. And you need this time to stay in good health more than anyone else.
- ❑ Balance your home responsibilities and career carefully, so that at no time does a guilt feeling overtake you. If you are feeling guilty, then maybe you need to talk it over with your immediate family, and if there is no resolution of the situation, professional advice is suggested.
- ❑ If you have a health problem, look into it. Seek professional advice. Ignoring it will not make it go away; it is likely to become worse. We realise you are busy, and hassled with innumerable problems, but at this point of time, your health is of utmost importance.
- ❑ Bring up your children in a way that they do not have to carry the yoke of age-old prejudices.
- ❑ Enjoy each passing day and keep some personal time for yourself.
- ❑ Bring the family together. Remember, it is your family, and one needs to be a part of a family to feel its bonding and its love.
- ❑ Do not waste time and energy over trivial matters. That time is well spent on introspection; you may arrive at conclusions that may surprise you!
- ❑ Hold yourself in the highest self-esteem; only then can you be the leader for your family.
- ❑ Remember, a mother is not one on whom you can lean on, but one who makes leaning unnecessary. Lead from the front.

I must share with you this little anecdote that never fails

to make me wonder at the wisdom of little children.

This little girl said, "Mother, I've had such a happy day today!"

"Really," her mother asked, "What made today different from yesterday?"

The child thought a moment and answered, "Yesterday my thoughts pushed me around and today I pushed my thoughts around."

Those words of a child picture life as it is. It shows a perpetual struggle between the things that push us around and the inner resources that enable us to push our life where it ought to go.

I give more emphasis on this section because the lady of the house in a quiet manner influences the thinking of the whole family. It is essential that she be in perfect physical, emotional and spiritual health to bring up a stress-free family.

> *Days in spite*
> *Of darkness, by the light*
> *Of a clear mind are day all night.*
> *Life, that dares send*
> *A challenge to her end,*
> *And when it comes, say, "Welcome, friend."*
> —R. Crawshaw

Welcome this challenge as a friend by being well prepared with all the tools at hand!

Physical health
Makes physical activity easy to perform

Promotes rest, relaxation, sleep and healing
Aids weight control
Contributes to nutritional health
Enhances disease resistance
Enhances accident resistance

Emotional and mental health

Strengthens resistance to emotional problems
Allows freedom from alcohol and drug abuse
Enhances self-esteem
Enhances ability to learn
Increases self-confidence

Social health

Provides social opportunities
Enhances intimate relationships
Opens the way for social and family support
Encourages family participation
Enhances energy for productive work

Spiritual health

Instills joy in life
Inspires courage to face challenges

I WILL OVERCOME!

Chapter 11
Overseas Stress

In the beginning we discussed how moving away from your house and familiar surroundings is a major   In

an uprooting of life not only from your known surroundings, but also to one of an alien culture. The job market has become such that openings are everywhere and the world

in 24 hours. Education has enabled us to cope with the

its emotions, cannot make the transition that quickly.

Not only for the traveller who is going, nay, gone, but also for the family who is left behind in a confused mess of emotions. Happiness over good career opportunities, happiness of material success, quixotic happiness that our boy is in the Silicon Valley, your heart missing the physical presence of the person, of seeing an empty chair at the dining table, of not being with him on his birthdays, and a thousand other little things.

For the young man who has moved on, the initial glamour, the excitement of a foreign land, the fears of being able to cope or not, of understanding the language and its nuances, and then the whammy! Missing home, missing mother running at your beck and call, missing home-cooked food, missing speaking your own native tongue, inability to cope with the smooth running of a household, longing for that dish that mum makes so well, nostalgia about Indian movies. The list is endless.

I have a vivid memory of some 15 years ago, when there was no e-mail, and telephone lines. At a concert of local Indian talent, a local doctor of adequate talent sang a new chartbuster currently on the popularity charts in India. The song was *"Chitthi aiyee hai"*, meaning "There is a letter from home." There wasn't a dry eye in the audience. Again, a year ago I heard another song, *"Sandese aate hain, hamein bulate hain, ke ghar kab aoge"*, saying, "Messages come from home, asking me when I will return?" And again, even with all the electronic communication that there is today, there wasn't a dry eye! Never mind the speed of the IT highway, the heart trudges along at its own pace; mostly coping with the new dimensions, but sometimes giving away to good old nostalgia. Elsewhere I mentioned spend your emotions. Have a good cry if you feel like it. And after the diversional tactic of a good cry, let us sit down to analyse the why's and whereof's of the situation.

Sarita came home extremely excited. In the spur of the moment, she accompanied her friend to a mass recruitment drive of some corporate companies for IT jobs. To her utter amazement, her experience and her capabilities prompted the headhunters to make her a good offer. She would be required to leave for the US in about a month's time on an assignment that could last about two years. Sarita's thoughts were a vivid montage of different and contrasting images. There was the sheer glamour of a foreign assignment, the temptation of big money, the fear of leaving her family and staying alone, the anxiety of leaving her children back; or could all of them move? Maybe, Vijay, an experienced scientist in the electronics field, can also manage to find a good job? Life would be beautiful. There would be lovely houses and lovely cars. All the nice things that the foreign-returned people turned up home with! And the children would get the benefit of excellent education, a lovely life and a great break in life! And they could pay off the house loan so fast. But who would care for Vijay's parents? In her mind, she found the solution. Ramesh is there, and he will get married, there will be another daughter-in-law in the house, and all will be well. This was too good a chance to miss.

The reaction in her home was equally excited. I guess dollar dreams surpass most realities. As it happened, Vijay was also eminently successful in landing a good post for himself in America, but in another city. He even managed to get the required lien from his department. Just in case he wanted to return to India, he wanted to have the security of his old job. All this made Anita and her husband also think in terms of foreign assignments. Ramesh was biding his time. If all his siblings were there, could he be far behind? Kamala, the matriarch of the family was the only one who would go into silent spells of contemplation. Her husband remained generally aloof, as if all this was not happening in his house. Sometimes, he would say, that now, the loan could be paid so easily, and he can die in peace in his ancestral house. Sometimes, he would sit simply gazing at the sky. All that was happening was so new and unexpected for the elderly couple. And soon it was departure time! Twenty-odd relatives stared at the jet till it banked over the sea and streaked the skies to distant lands. The telephone call of safe arrival came from a jetlagged Vijay and his family from California, and the Surendranath's heaved a sigh of relief.

And then came the sounds of silence. The elderly couple missed the children tremendously. While this was outwardly evident and openly expressed, they also missed the presence of Vijay and Sarita. They not only missed the little things they did for them, but missed them, as you miss a part of your body, mind and heart. They knew that all was well with their son and his family, and they would do well, but how do you convince your enigmatic heart, a heart that has its own reasons? Slowly, ever so slowly, stress accumulated, and with it, the already present hypertension increased. Visits to the doctors became more frequent, and an insipient anxiety and depression settled over the elderly couple. With it came morbid thoughts like, "Who will look after us if we fall ill? Will Vijay even be able to come in time to cremate me when I die?"

The telephone calls cheered them up sometimes, but many a time, left a larger longing to feel, to touch, to be with them. Depression, so common in the elderly, firmly took root, and unfortunately was left untreated as it was something one had to accept. Depression was for the weak minded, and all that was required was "will power" to get above the situation. Sleeplessness? That was a common complaint with the elderly. They just need lesser amount of sleep. Morbid thoughts? Well, it was the beginning of the end, wasn't it? A clinician would diagnose this as depression; depression that could so easily be managed as easily as one would treat hypertension, if only one took the pains to get over a mindset and visit the doctor.

Doctors in India have a new dimension to their work these days. We have children of our patients call us long distance enquiring after the health of their parents, and assuring us that we were free to make the best of treatment available to them, as there was absolutely no problem with expenses. This is a positive gesture, and generally reassures the parents to some extent. However, it is not the solution, and coping skills need to be practised. Possibly, because of the age factor, some help from psychiatrists may be helpful. I would request children living abroad to speak to their parents about the good of counselling, and while they are at it, to convince parents that psychiatrists are not the next thing to the doctors for mad people; that as they would consult a cardiologist for a heart problem, a psychiatrist is to be consulted for coping with the problems.

Let us now leave India or Pakistan or Bangladesh—why, it may well be the same in Korea, Philippines or Mexico—or wherever people are leaving their homelands to settle in a new milieu; to land in the land of milk and honey, today's utopia, the United States of America.

Vijay and Sarita or anyone of his or her ilk is facing a fair share of situations that require quick adapting skills. A whole new setup, especially for those who were not previously exposed to foreign travel or who come from a multitude of small towns and villages of the subcontinent, a new work culture where one has to prove his or her skills unlike the lackadaisical attitude to jobs in India, coping with the house and housekeeping without household help, helping children to fit in new surroundings, and, as with their parents back home, a sense of tremendous nostalgia for all the things back home. Being younger, and equipped with the determination to do something good with their lives, and really lacking in time to brood too much, the younger generation copes slightly better than the older ones they leave behind.

Some of them, with time, that is a couple of decades, adapt to a curious eclectic culture that shifts tracks as and when required from the adapted American to the quintessential Indian! Even in these so-called "well adapted" people, there are times for concern and intense introspection. This is most often when they consider the marriages of their children. I suspect that their heart pulls them to an Indian alliance, while the saner mind tells them that for a child raised totally in the West, such an alliance has little chances of working out. I suspect there are minor issues too, like food habits, particularly with the disparity of the cuisine at home and that served at school, dress codes that differ vehemently from those of their parents, manners and traditions that the elders feel the children need to abide by, while to the children all this is so dramatically alien. I have seen times of intense squabbling when it is time for the prom evenings. I have witnessed parents in tears when their children ask them why it is wrong to go out on a date, or why they can't take up a job elsewhere and leave home and live independently.

I am only quoting a few examples; all of you are familiar with the scenario. Each family has its own particular coping problems, why each person has his own problems; there are no solutions, except to learn to ask what exactly you want from life, and then go about it systematically; asking for, and seeking help for yourself and for the loved ones left behind in your native lands. Above all, let distance not take away from that all-important attribute, TLC. Even across the wires, TLC can and should be administered. Do not wait for the Mother's days and Father's days, or whatever else ambitious salespersons may come up with, but make some time, regularly, to keep in touch. For the uninitiated, TLC means *tender loving care*. Money is not the substitute for TLC. But like they say, money can make the tough times a little easier. Help your parents feel comfortable even if you are not there to look after them. Help them cope with their concerns regarding their health. You know best what hassles your family. A few words on the phone, a letter, or an e-mail for the computer savvy will hopefully reduce the distance between the hearts.

A special word of concern. Do not feel guilty, and do not let anyone make you feel guilty that you have left your parents in their old age. In a world of love and care, which I hope you are all a part of, there is no place for such negative feelings. Being the nurturing individual that you are, and the caring person your parent put an effort to bring up, there is no place on either side for such unwanted burdens.

Work towards coping with your emotions, and go out of your way to help your loved ones at home to cope.

It is now time for some introspection. For each of us to ponder over these questions, and just maybe, a clearer picture will emerge; possibly, things will not look so bleak, and probably, you will come to believe that there was never a problem in the first place. It was just a matter of looking at things from a different angle!

Some thoughts for the parents of children who live abroad.

1. What did you aspire for your children? A good career anywhere in the world, or you never really ever wanted them to leave your side?
2. Do you accept that they are adults and need to make their own choices? That it is the time to metaphorically cut the umbilical cord?
3. Precisely what do you expect from your children in your old age?
   —Caring
   —Material/financial security
   —Physical proximity and the assurance that they will be with you when you need them
4. Do you genuinely believe that their living in the same place will solve all your problems? That their living in Mumbai instead of Boston would matter if you are in any case living in Kolkata?
5. Are you particularly concerned about ill health and whether there will be any caregivers at your bedside?
6. Have you heard about the "empty nest syndrome," or is what you are feeling simple and plain "retirement blues"? A period of ennui that you are blaming on your children being away?
7. Do you make efforts to cultivate your own circle of

friends/relatives who can foster a feeling of caring amongst yourselves?

8. Do you make an effort to cultivate a hobby like reading, walking, meeting friends or support group activity in the community to keep you in a "feel good mood"? One may consider music recitals, religious discourses, walking groups in the neighbourhood, and for the more energetic, participation in a civic activity like mobilising support to help clean your area, writing to the press, etc.

9. If you are not interested in any of the above, and feel incapable mentally to think of some activity that makes you feel good, would you consider talking to a counsellor/psychologist?

10. Do you enjoy communicating with your children abroad? Little notes of happiness, of events in the neighbourhood, a movie you saw, or a recent book you read? Or are letters meant only to communicate your "problems", "sufferings", and "difficulties",—real or perceived?

11. Do you look forward to your holidays abroad with your children or are you more bothered about the hassles of the long journey, the alien surroundings when you get there, about how lonely you feel there, how there is no one to talk to, that you cannot go out on your own, that your children work long hours, that your grandchildren practically talk another language you really cannot understand?

12. Would you want to make an attempt to observe/learn how the rest of the world lives? Would you want to look for some interesting things in the lifestyle of a new country?

13. Do you tell your grandchildren happy stories of your childhood, of your life and times, of their

country of origin, and do you ask them to tell you about their friends, their various activities?
14. Are you genuinely happy with the success your children have achieved in another country, or would you rather feel happy when they gave it all up and came back home to you?
15. Are you willing to consider that in today's rapidly changing world, your children, their children and you need to be willing to accept some change as a way of life, and to do so with a cheerful disposition rather than a burdensome task thrust upon you?

Now, here are some introspective questions for the generation that has moved on to a new country. You have a satisfying career; you are really busy coping with the many obligations of job and family. And yes, you need to unwind, you need your vacation time, you cannot always be thinking of your family back home. I would still like you to go through these questions—it could help.

1. Do you make time to call home at specified and predetermined intervals of your choice? Remember, a reasonably fixed schedule cuts down on your parents' anxiety levels and removes a feeling of perpetual waiting. Additional calls are pleasant surprises, are always welcome and add to that feel-good experience. The generation you are dealing with has grown up being very brief and business-like on the phone; they need to be encouraged to open up and have a normal conversation as if one is face-to-face rather than treat the telephone as a business tool.
2. Do you send pictures, inform your family of positive career developments or cite pressures of work and a busy schedule as an excuse to get away from these things?
3. Do you reassure your parents that you are always there for them in their time of need—as in when there is a major crisis—or do you believe that this is something they should "know" and

need not be reiterated often?
4. Do you reassure your parents that you will look after them in their old age; or are you helping out even now in your own way?
5. Would you consider making a definite financial arrangement for your parents so that they will not need to ask you specifically when they are in need? In short, would you consider giving them some financial security?
6. Do you visit your family in your country at least once every couple of years?
7. Would you like your parents to spend time with you in your home every couple of years?
8. Do you let them enjoy the occasional benefit of the original dollar dream—like time and effort-saving gadgets in the house, some repairs that you finance, a new set of tyres for the old family car, sending them on a pilgrimage/holiday that they have always dreamt of?
9. When they visit you, do you make time to be with them, take them around, introduce them to your friends or leave them on their own. Or worse, feel uncomfortable about their lack of social and language skills and prefer to keep them in seclusion?
10. Do you look upon them as nurturing grandparents to be left in charge of grandchildren, or as a free alternative to the local day care?
11. Do you encourage parents to develop new hobbies/skills or put them down as "too old" for that sort of thing?
12. If you have observed signs of anxiety/stress/depression, would you lovingly convince them to see a counsellor? Or would you dismiss it as typical of old age and ignore it?
13. Do you reassure them that being in another

country does not alter family ties and affections, and could, in fact, augment the help they would have otherwise found difficult to give.

14. Do you suffer from a guilt trip for living abroad, marrying out of your community and other such things?
15. Do you sit and talk to your parents that in this brave new world all of you have to collectively make some adjustments and some compromises based on love and a need to change rather than a coercion to adapt?

While I have some reservations about the use of the word "quality time" when referring to little children, when both the protagonists are adults, I genuinely advocate the allotment of quality time in the family—be it on the phone, if not person-to-person.

I have asked many people the question if they could sit down for an uninterrupted half an hour with their son/daughter in the house. The answer was in the negative. Across the continents, on the phone lines, on chat networks, believe me, it is possible.

I am for quality time.

"All happy families resemble one another; every unhappy family is unhappy in its own way."

— *Tolstoy, Anna Karenina*

Chapter 12
Stress and Retirement

Howdy, old-timer. I heard you were telling you are getting

bored with it. You keep mumbling that you are not good for anything any more, just because there is snow on your roof. Well, let me tell you a thing or two about old age.

Vanderbilt at eighty added more then $100 million to his fortune. Thiers at seventy-three established the French

stone became premier of England for the fourth time at eighty-three. Wordsworth earned the laureateship at seventy-three. Verdi wrote "Falstaff" at eighty. Stradi-

through his own efforts, he paid that amount in full and built a lasting reputation.

Now, shake hands and refocus your attention and stay with it one way or the other until the end."

—*Oren Arnold*

We have our own list of eminent people to add to this

politicians to social workers, from artists of great eminence to poets and authors.

Yet, the common man is often heard bemoaning his retirement, of how useless he feels, and how time hangs on his hands! Many family doctors and families have found that these post-retirement blues have often led to heart attacks in seemingly healthy individuals. Which means that retirement in itself is a major *stressor*!

Let us take a close look at what retirement means, what it does to the individual and his family, and how choices can be made constructively.

What does retirement mean to most people? While it is a landmark inasmuch that it means the effective end of your working life, it has numerous unsaid but implied emotions that go with it. The first thing a retired individual's experiences is that he has time hanging on his hands. The second thing he realises is that he is missing the environment, the ambience of the workplace, the camaraderie of senior officers, the feeling of being the captain of the ship. The third issue that is sometimes the biggest one is that he will no longer receive a paycheck at the end of the month. The fourth issue is more an emotional one than the others, and is often subjective—he perceives that the family is no longer giving him the status he has been used to, and he believes that he is considered a hindrance in the house; he is in the house all day long, and the family is really not used to this situation and treats him as an interloper. While all of these may not apply to each and every one, some of the factors will probably apply to most of the retired people.

It is often said that plans for retirement should begin the day a person joins his first job. While this may sound pessimistic, it actually suggests that various life events can be planned so that retirement is generally without too many tensions. Starting from planning your wedding to having your first child, everything has a meaning in the larger scheme of things. Then one goes on to planning the building of your own home/apartment at a suitable time so that repayment of loans can finish before retirement. The reason for marriage and bearing children at an appropriate time and age is because in our country, the "settling" of children in jobs and marriages is very much considered to be the responsibility of the parents. This being so, if one has married late and his children are born when he is well into his 40s it is unlikely that he could have settled his children before his retirement. That is not to say that such individuals may not have made some very viable plans for each contingency in their lives, but we are talking of the lowest common denominator and not the cases that have planned well.

Along with this goes the question of financial planning. I am sure everyone has his own concept of his necessities and obligations. This is just a reminder that it is wise to begin planning early in life. I have so often seen people put away plans of retirement saying that "it is a long way off", and before you know it, the day has come with its myriad adjustments!

While it may be possible to effectively plan financial details of one's life when one works with considerable foresight (but do we?), getting used to the question of time hanging on one's hands, and missing the ambience or sometimes the trappings of one's previous position, is easier said than done. In India, the date of retirement of most employees is given, and hardly varies at the most by two years. That means everyone knows when exactly they are to retire. While some make appropriate decisions about doing some courses which may offer them other employment, most prefer to play along and take things as they come. Others may make some sort of a start in other fields, and while some succeed, the odds are against most seniors in this rapidly changing world. The methods of working, the old world courtesies, the rapid advancement of technology into most fields, make the retired person rather lost in the new environment. A sense of being "useless" prevails. Slowly and slowly, this could develop into a mild form of depression.

Some officers, particularly those in government service, find that they hugely miss the trappings of the post they held prior to retirement. The other family members also feel deprived. If one had "got done with responsibilities" as perceived by us in India, it is easier to get used to the new situation.

We now come to the whimsical situation of family members finding this "new" person in the house the whole day, and not knowing how to deal with it. I have heard some amusing stories of wives complaining as to how her husband interferes in all her housekeeping duties and consequently, neither is the work done nor the dreams of easy companionship in old age seem to materialise. Some have gone so far as to remark that their husbands seem to have undergone a metamorphosis and are perceptibly "different" people! Here we come across tragic–comic situations where the man feels that by virtue of his experience in the outside world, he knows best, and the lady feels that this is her domain, and she is the boss! The husband who says that he makes the decisions about all major issues like how much the World Bank should advance to our country, or when the lending rate of the Reserve Bank should decrease, while his wife makes all the smaller decisions like when to buy a washing machine or where to go for their annual holiday is indeed a happy retired couple!

With this feeling of helplessness and somewhat feeling alien in their own houses comes the feeling that the rest of the household is no longer treating him as the most important person, the *in situ* head of the family, but as an "also ran". This could be a mistaken perception, or occasionally, it could be that the reins have been handed over willy-nilly into the new incumbents hands—be it your own child. The decision making is now the prerogative of the new incumbent, and the old head of the family is just that—the old head of the family.

"The old order changeth, yielding place to the new", is immortalised in Tennyson's poetry and more appropriately, I venture to suggest Thoreau's line—

"Things do not change; we do. Or, we should!"

It is essential that we absorb all changes without prejudice and without being judgmental and effectively retire to the status from Queen to the King's mother!

At this juncture nothing can work but calling to mind the entire repertoire of possible things to do to while away time. Again, one has to fall back on skills acquired in one's youth—be it writing, painting, gardening, cooking or anything else. Of course, the more adventurous can begin to learn a new craft—I personally know of an enterprising senior citizen who went on to do her PhD after her retirement. While not all of us can be so magnificently venturesome, it is not a bad idea to develop some hobbies that one has carefully tucked away in some corner of the brain in a category marked, "I shall do this when I retire." The spectrum can extend from playing the stock market to educating children living in the nearby slum. Teach man his own; as long as he is passing his time fruitfully. I shall pause to add a caveat here. Gambling or drinking away the whole day at local clubs can hardly qualify as an acceptable activity. On the other hand, if one is looking at the factor of self-esteem or rather the loss of it, such indulgences will only accelerate ones downfall. Yes, the day will not be far when your family considers you a liability rather than the respected head of the household.

Let us consider Surendranath's attitude to his retirement.

Yes, he had married at the proper time, and could get his daughter married while still working, and also his older son has completed his studies, got a good job and is happily married. However, Surendranath had to take a mortgage on his house towards the end of his career, and is now somewhat bogged down with the repayments from his pension. He often wishes that his son Vijay took over this burden. He also finds time hanging on his hands, has no particular hobbies except reading the paper thoroughly, reading a few books and watching a few television programmes. This is however a bone of contention. Various family members have their own favourite programmes, and no one is willing to concede to grandfather's seniority. It is the other way round—since the grandfather is at home always, he can watch television at other times! Surendranath has a few friends who visit him once in a while or whom he visits sometimes, but this most often is confined to family functions like weddings and such.

Fortunately, he has no gambling instincts, and though he occasionally reminisces about the old times, he is content enough to spend time with his family. He does not try to be "helpful" in the kitchen and infringe on his wife's terrain. He is typically Indian in his perceptions, and would not dream of entering the kitchen—in fact, he would be totally helpless if his wife and others were to be out of town for a family wedding! In his youth, he had played badminton and was wondering whether he should attempt to take up the game again. His family felt that at his age, it can lead to medical problems and it is better that he confined himself to a more sedate activity. However, when he developed high blood pressure, his daughter-in-law, Sarita encouraged him to take up the game. He now spends an hour every evening in the courts. He has consequently made new friends, and the evening passes away happily. Psychologists have found that an active and productive life generally keeps heart problems away.

He is, however, troubled that his younger son, Ramesh is yet to finish his education and has a niggling fear about his future. In a bid to help him settle and also to ease his existing problem of his mortgage, Surendranath went on a job-hunting spree. He hardly found any openings, and when he did, he found that he was working "under" what he called, children younger than his son! He was not happy with the situation, and neither did he find the computerised systems of accounting comfortable. He quit, and remained depressed for some time. He started worrying a lot.

Seeing him upset, his wife Kamala felt very helpless and frustrated. She had always been a homemaker, and as such had no retirement problems—homemakers or housewives, as they were called, never retire! They continue to plod along and surprisingly, are the last ones to complain of retirement problems. She began to wonder if she can put her culinary skills to use, and in this world of entrepreneurship, whether she can start a catering business on a small scale. Hasn't this been advocated so often on the television? Her sons opposed the idea vehemently with the argument, "What will everyone say? That we are not looking after you that you need to work at this age?" Her husband too was not for it. Anyways, Kamala's desire to pitch in was not because she was bored and had nothing to do, but to help ease her husband's tensions. Sarita's and Vijay's foreign assignment put paid to these plans, and the Surendranaths settled down to a retired but somewhat boring life—they missed their grandchildren.

Anxiety about one's health is a major *stressor* in a senior citizen's life. It is best to take such precautions as one can, like sensible food habits, exercise, sound sleep, attending promptly to medical problems so that they do not escalate, taking prescribed medicines on time and having a total medical check-up once a year. Worrying about health is hardly beneficial; one needs to be proactive when there is a problem and not indulge in "ifs and buts" or imaginary scenarios in the absence of problems—the syndrome of, "What will happen if I get cancer like my neighbour?"

A walk a day keeps the doctor away, and a smile a day keeps worry away!

What will retirement be for you? For each of the following questions, choose the answer that describes as nearly as possible your expectations.

1. How fit do you expect to be at 60?
    a. I expect to be less fit than I am now.
    b. I expect to be very fit for my age.

2. What will be your financial status?
    a. I expect to be financially dependent on my family.
    b. I expect to be financially independent.

3. How many friends will you have in your social circle?
    a. I will have only a few friends or none.
    b. I will have many friends.

4. What sort of things will you do with your friends?
    a. I won't do much of anything with my friends.
    b. I expect to enjoy many varied activities with my friends.

5. What will be your state of mind?
    a. I will be set in my ways.
    b. I will be happy, cheerful and curious.

Scoring. Your answers not only reveal what you will probably be in your older years, but also what you think of elder people.

If you have five "b" answers, your attitude is consistent with a rewarding and fulfilling later life.

If you have four or even three "b" answers, you will be a happy individual for the most part, but you can try to prepare for your senior years in a more participative way.

If your "b" answers are lesser than three, you unfortunately have some ageist prejudices that may adversely affect the quality of your later years.

My guess would be that most often people do suffer from some inbuilt prejudices, sown in childhood and nurtured during the growing years. Very few of our senior citizens make a determined effort to enjoy life and rather make a habit of comparing situations and things with "their times"—often unfavourably, and being critical of things, events, people of today. Yes, "I am set in my ways, and cannot change," describes their attitude best. One gets the impression that underlying depression makes them so critical of things, and generally rather irritating to deal with. One can hardly expect anyone to converse with you if you are nothing but critical of his opinions! I would suggest that the concerned individual or his immediate family notice the change in temperament of the individual, and gently talk to him, try to involve him in various duties, talks, even games, and if that is not possible, I suggest some professional help. It could be that some medicines can bring about a dramatic change in their outlook. It should be recognised that being depressed has nothing to do with "lack of will power", and like excess of sugar causes diabetes, the lack of a chemical in the brain called "serotonin" causes depression.

At the other end of the spectrum, we have elderly persons who are so full of life and are eager to do new things, to be active, and have a very non-supportive and abrasive family who makes disparaging remarks like, "Why can't he behave his age?" or "Why does he need to spend time and money on his enjoyment rather than sit at home and read some religious books?" The senior citizen has every right to enjoy his life as he wants to—I have already mentioned some caveats. The underlying principle being that no action of any individual should be abrasive and not in keeping with the norms of the society in which he is living. It is time that elders are encouraged to develop hobbies, seek the company friends of their age and have group activities together.

In this section, the retired individual has been portrayed as a man, and problems discussed as pertaining to him. Looking around, I find, and you will agree with me, that women are more adaptable to new situations in their life than men are. Also, generally the duties of running and managing a house, plus the involvement as caregivers of grandchildren keeps their time pretty much occupied. Also, by nature, they tend to make more friends, be it the neighbour across the road or a childhood classmate, and tend to keep in touch with just plain chatting sessions, keep relationships alive. This gives them a chance to not only fill in their spare time, but also ventilate such problems that they might have. There are instances of established career women finding the initial phase unsettling, but it is known that women cope better with retirement than men do.

It is so easy for me to write these words, you say. I agree. But unless a beginning is made, an effort is made, a change is made, can we hope to better things? We must make a change.

In whatever senior citizens attempt to do for their happiness, or youngsters encourage their elders to participate in, the standard should be:

> *"The logic of worldly success rests on a fallacy: the strange error that our perfection depends on the thoughts and opinions and applause of other men!"*
>
> — *Thomas Merton*

And lastly,

> *To me — old age is always fifteen years older than I am!*
>
> — *Bernard Shaw*

Chapter 13
Stress and Superstition

This section never existed in the planning stage. When friends came to know that I was planning 13 chapters, they were aghast! How can one start off with such an inauspicious number! After all, even in developed

said. And slowly, I realised how susceptible we are to superstition, and how such inexplicable entities can play on your psyche. Every country has its share of superstitions; some harmless and easy to live by, some harmless and easy to live by, some more exhausting in

it appears that they play on the mind. And anything that plays on the mind, eventually becomes a stressor. Do it and be damned, do not do it and be equally damned!

"If you are distressed by anything external, the pain is not due to the thing itself, but due to your estimate of it; and this you have the power to revoke at any moment", said Marcus Aurelius.

Superstitions are these external factors that trouble you; and worse, even if you are inherently not bothered by them, others continually stress on them and you begin to categorise them as the harbingers of good fortune if you comply, and bodings of ill tidings if you do not. The quantum of stress exerted by these totally uncalled for situations is tremendous.

I shall not enumerate superstitions except to cite one or

two to illustrate how they can be *stressors*. I will leave it to your imagination and intellect to interpret any superstitions that you are prone to come across and, of course, to exert your choices. This book is, after all, to emphasise that life is full of choices!

Surendranaths had some tough choices before them. Their daughter was born under an inauspicious star—one of those where by tradition, all sorts of ills befall the family into which this girl is married. Kamala had spent a large part of her life under the duress of this superstition. When they began to search for a suitable bridegroom, they faced a lot of refusals. Fortunately, they did find an engineer whose family was willing to overlook this so-called negative attribute. Anita was married, however, her parents spent many a tension-filled day worrying whether this marriage would have any negative manifestations in her marital home. They made special efforts to appease her in-laws by being liberal with presents whenever the occasion demanded—and there are many—and were also very protective of their daughter Anita; they did not want her to suffer in any way. Two years into the marriage, and Anita has not yet been able to start a family. The Surendranaths worry whether it is the curse of the star she was born under.

You can well imagine the stress this family is under, in spite of marrying their daughter into an understanding family that does not pay any heed to such matters. Anita and her husband sometimes worry that some distant relation or friend may sow the seed of this superstition in their family. All their life, the Surendranaths went through every sort of religious ceremony purported to appease the stars. While it is essential to concede that more things are brought by prayer than this world dreams of, this family could have well done without the stress of this issue for all those years. They do not believe that the sword of Damocles' is away from them even now.

Stress and Superstition

Life has it's own way of throwing challenges. Just when Surendranath breathed a sigh of relief that Anita's wedding went off without a hitch, Ramesh faced problems with his college education. Advice came in from all sides. One of the significant ones was where it was pointed out that the master bedroom in the house was facing the wrong direction, and structural changes to that room could well be the harbinger of good times and tidings. Surendranath was flabbergasted. He had just mortgaged his house so as to meet the wedding expenses, and here were well-wishers telling him that he needed to make significant structural changes. This was his ancestral house, and his parents had built it some 50 years ago. He remembered his childhood days; while there were some difficult times, on the whole, he recollected that life was uncomplicated and good. Then suddenly where did this unsuitable architecture spring up? From the extra room that was added some 20 years ago, when he was newly married. Apparently, this altered the "balance" of the house.

Surendranath was confused. He was also very tense. But he had some very visible problems. Even if he wanted to make the alterations, he was strapped for cash; he was very near retirement, had used up most of his provident fund advances, taken a mortgage, and dared not use any more of his frugal resources as he largely depended upon them after his retirement. In a ripple effect, the tension was passed down to the whole family; tempers ran high, and visits to the doctors began eating into their resources. It is possible that he would have begged or borrowed the money for the alterations when yet another of his ilk told him that a simple alteration of the doorframe could well be sufficient. Literally thanking his stars, Surendranath hurriedly got it done. Problem solved. At least the family breathed easy, and whether it was because of the change in the position of the door or just the relief from tension, things began to get back on even keel.

I have heard of numerous instances when a potential employee had to do an interview or start on a journey on a so-called inauspicious day. Whatever may be the outcome otherwise, the approach itself is under strained circumstances, sort of under a cloud. Believers are put under immense stress when faced with such situations. This could adversely affect their performance.

The aim of this section is not to discuss or dissect the good or bad of such events, neither to criticise nor coerce people away from their beliefs. It is to highlight that these situations are potentially great *stressors*, particularly when they are occurring time and again or where there is great expense to be borne. There are no solutions except that you are armed with the knowledge that you are in a tough spot. Possibly, some diversionary tactic, or physical exercise can help you cope with your original problem (plus the one created by the stress of the superstition), or yoga could do the trick!

Like I said, I have moved away from my original plan to accommodate this section!

Chapter 14
Stress at Workplace

Workplace stress is the harmful physical and emotional response which occurs if there is a poor match between job demands and the capabilities, resources available or the needs of the workers. Stress is a prevalent and costly problem in today's workplace. High levels of stress is reported by about one-third of the workers. Stress at the workplace is considered to be a major stressor in the lives of more than one quarter of the employees. Stress at workplace has been a major cause of turnover in every organisation.

Causes

Stress at workplace comes up due to several problems such as misplacement of paper or tools, low salary, failure of machinery or equipment including computer system, labour distances, personality clashes, incompetent subordinates or boss, complaints arising due to many reasons, boring work, bad environment, sexual harassment, negative attitude of management, lack of proper social security to employees, absence of incentives for the highest achieved targets, and various other job-related pressures.

Job stress results from interaction. The views differ as the characteristics of workers versus money conditions is the primary cause of job stress. The differing viewpoints suggest different ways to prevent stress at work. Infact, diffences in individual characteristics such as personality and skills are very significant in predicting whether certain jobs conditions will result in stress. So to say, What is stressful for one person may not be a problem for someone else. This viewpoint underlies prevention strategies which works on workers and also the ways to help them cope with demanding job conditions.

The importance of individuals diffrences cannot be ignored and scientific evidence suggests that certain working conditions are stressful for most people. This kind of evidence argues that more emphasis should be given on the working conditions as the main source of job stress. It suggests that job redesign is the primary prevention strategy. A person's status in the workplace can also affect levels of stress. While workplace stress has the potential to affect employees of various categories, it has also been seen that the employees who have less control over their jobs are more likely to suffer from stress than powerful managers.

With the use of upgraded technology and other communication revolutions, the computers have become more efficient and productive. This increase in productivity has been linked to increased stress levels among the employess due to higher expectations and greater competition. This is giving rise to stress faced by the employess because of economic factors in the 21st Century. Such economic stress also develops due to pressure from investors as they can quickly withdraw money from company stocks or because of lack of trade and professional unions.

Signs

Stress-related disorders ecompass a broad group of conditions such as depression, anxiety, post-traumatic stress disorder, dissatisfaction, fatique, tension, substance abuse, lack of concentration, anger, fear, frustration, confusion, boredom, hatred, panic, shame, embarrassment, mood changes, disturbed sleep upset stomach, headaches, cardiovascular disease and problems in relationships with family and friends. The effects of job stress on chronic diseases are more difficult to ascertain because these are influenced by various factors other than stres. Stress at workplace also results in unusual behaviours and symptoms like rudeness, forgetting things indicating loss of memory, social withdrawal, absenteeism, arguments, avoidance, day dreaming, etc. Job stress is also associated with many biological reactions ultimately leading to compromised health, which in turn results in poor work performance, efficiency and low productivity.

Prevention

As discussed, workplace stress is very harmful and affects the efficiency of employees and ultimatly the productivity. To prevent stress at work, a combination of oragnisational changes and stress management is very important. The most useful approach is as follows:

- Worker's roles and responsibilities should be clearly defined.
- Workers should be provided with opportunities to interact.
- Workload is to be ensured to the workers as per their capabilities and resources.
- Jobs for the workers should be designed in such a way that the same provide them with the opportunity to use their skills.
- Workers should be given opportunities to participate in making decisions that affect their jobs.
- Communication skills of workers should be improved for their career development.

- ❏ Avoid discrimination at workplace based an gender, origin, religion or language.
- ❏ Take advice of an objective outsider or a consultant for persistant problems.
- ❏ Participative leadership style should be introduced to involve as many subordinates as possible to solve stress-producing problems.

Chapter 15
Stress and your Financial Portfolio

Financial stress is sadly, a widespread experience. See how it affects you and what you can do. According to a survey, roughly 7 in 10 respondents are extremely stressed about money whereas 1 in 10 report that they are not

about money is only going up. This is because of the fact

as depression and sleep disturbance. With the increase in cost of gas, food and other essential commodities besides

and tension over money is negatively affecting health in many ways.

Unhealthy habits: people are experiencing a lot of

overeating and other unhealthy, coping behaviours.

due to lack of

crisis, and tend to cut down on the expenses of health so as to pay for food and other basic necessities. Thus small problems turn into big ones.

Sleep disturbance:
experience troubled sleep, impaired immune functioning and cognitive abilities, causing additional problems.

Credit emotions: people start buying most of the things

against credit cards. They experience anxiety, frustration and feelings of hopelessness as the debt piles up. An additional amount of money is to be paid as interest. This causes further stress.

It is no wonder that financial stress is felt in every corner of the world. Even the Americans are not spared. The following are some resources to help in handling your financial situation and to reduce stress to build a more secure future:

See where you stand: find out if you have a major money problem or your situation is under control. Ask yourself such questions and see how much help you require to get on the right track.

System that can help you: find out the budget that suits your lifestyle and gives you financial satisfaction.

Get out of debt: try to get out of credit card debt. Make it a habit to buy anything against cash payment. That would keep your budget within limit as per the money in your pocket.

Save money and cut costs: make it a habit to save, taking it as essential expenditure. On the other hand, try to cut costs while spending money which is also as good as saving.

Moreover, frequent news keeps pouring in from the government, especially news pertaining to increase in petrol, diesel, LPG, and CNG prices overnight, causing financial strain to the common man's monthly budget. The budget of the house is suddenly disturbed with by the modern trend of inflation. With the increase in petrol price, the cost of all the essential commodities is automatically enhanced. The government does not increase the salaries of the people proportionately with the result that the public goes under severe financial stress with more taxes imposed every year other than the sudden announcements during the year.

Political uncertainties also induce financial stress because in certain cases the traders keep on increasing the price but in those conditions the government does not have any interest. The ruling government is likely to go and the new government takes time to take over.

It is not only internal political uncertainties but the global economy that affects the common man. The economies of America, Europe and the Gulf countries play an important role. Any problem in the American economy disturbs the entire world. Any disturbance in oil-producing countries brings rise in the price of crude oil which affects the economy of all the countries. If there is an increase in the price of oil in the international market, the inflation boils everywhere. So financial stress is caused due to not only internal sources but also due to external ones.

Chapter 16

Stress between Husband and Wife

It is commonly seen that stress due to some or the other reason prevails between husband and wife, irrespective of

peacefully right from the day they get married till death.

between husband and wife is devastating not only for a marriage but for the entire family. The stress it causes the family unit can have lasting effects. A feasible way

Do you feel the stress, tension, anxiety or anger due to your spouse makes you afraid that your marriage is heading towards divorce which you cannot stop? Are you worried that your spouse is going to quit on your relationship and you are not able to do anything about it? Then it is time to frame out some changes and start working to imporve your marriage which you think is in trouble. Get started to end your relationship troubles. You must go for

build on that. It will certainly show you as to how to view

thereby providing a healthy path of moving forward.

Before getting started you must make sure that you are serious to front forth the effort that will help to save your marriage. The task that lies ahead of you is no easy. You must try very hard to get over the feelings of hurt and only has to be overcome but has to be let go of mentally. Prepare yourself to really work hard at rescuing your marriage and only then the problems would be sorted out. Commit to working on making it better.

There are numerous things that you can get started on and move in the right direction. Such information will be invaluable in really providing the help and also the insight to make lasting and permanent changes. You have to act as briefed here.

1. Make a firm commitment to stay married. Recollect your wedding day and vows you made. Remember those promises which were a moral commitment to each other through all kinds of situations. Never consider divorce as an option.
2. You have to act lovingly towards your spouse though you may not feel like doing so. It is infact the hardest thing to do, but you have to forget everything that happened in the past.
3. Start communicating positively with your spouse and take out time to listen to him. Begin with small talk and work your way up. This will come more easily if you have implemented to act lovingly towards your spouse. This will bring you closer to your spouse day-by-day.
4. You have to stop complaining and start complimenting. This decision will not only let positive remarks escape your lips but will do good too. Initially it may be hard to do but the more you do it, the more naturally it would come. After that you would be able to reciprocate the comments positively to your spouse. Always focus on positive attitude. This is a change in perspective that comes with acting lovingly towards your spouse.
5. You should be willing to forgive as you know that nobody is perfect. Holding on to your anger only makes you more angry. Justice need not always be

served whereas mercy and compassion can always be given.

6. You should be willing to compromise. You are not always right. One person is responsible for the behaviour that starts a fight while the other person is responsible for the reaction to that behaviour. It takes two to fight.

7. Try to have more fun together. You used to enjoy each other's company. What was it like then? Try that again and see how it positively works to regain your marriage.

8. Sometimes your spouse may have a doubt about your relationship with someone else. So it is always better to clarify such things at the earliest. The more you hide or delay, the more thick it becomes. Once you come out with the facts frankly, the matter gets diluted. Thereafter such problems gradually vanish with the lapse of time. You should always stick to declaring the affair as merely friendship and while doing so, your statements should be brief. The more you elaborate on things, the more easily you would be misunderstood and it would become very difficult for you to save your marriage. This is a very sensitive point and you have to tackle it very diplomatically.

9. You have the option to seek help of a trained marriage counsellor. At times you need a third party to help you out, to give you a clear picture of what is really going on. Don't hestitate in getting such help and rather it is wise to get such help. This way you get the appropriate advice too.

10. Discover the secret to save your marriage. Try to learn the proven methods for getting your marriage back on track. Good communication with your spouse is the first step to regain your marriage. If you are struggling to communicate with your spouse it would be better to work on it to get positive

results. Conflicts may arise between you and your spouse because of poor communication skills. Bad communication certainly destroys a marriage and many a times you are not even able to recognise that you are communicating poorly with your spouse. So communication with your spouse has to be improved to save your marriage.

11. The foundations of good communication can be outlined as follows:
    i. Listening- If you listen to your spouse carefully you communicate then to your spouse that they are important.
    ii. Understanding – You have to give feedback to your spouse that you have clearly understood what he was talking about. Your appreciation towards whatever your spouse said would enhance your relations with positive attitude.

Apart from good communication with your spouse there are some other things to do such as replace criticism with praise, blaming with understanding, talking with listening, defensiveness with openness, and silence with sharing. These things, if implemented, will bring excellent results to save your marriage.

The next important decision is to remove divorce as an option. Many a times the conflict between you and your spouse becomes ugly. Even an intensive tension can be diffused if you take divorce off the table. If your marriage is seeming troubled that means you are considering divorce. Instead, you can try alternate therapies such as marriage counselling or even communication. Whichever way you go, don't bring divorce as an option. It has been observed that those who deny divorce as an option and are committed to a marriage, will certainly be more motivated to work on that marriage and find an end to the problem.

Chapter 17
Stress and Illness

In today's life, everyone experiences some kind of stress in one or other form. Daily we come in contact with billions of germs and each of them is capable of bringing about illness which may prove fatal. It is not neccessary that everyone who comes in contact with germs falls ill. It looks like some people are totally immune to contracting any type of illness, while many people are so sensitive that they become ill just at the mere thought of germs. They infact act like a magnet for illness and become ill even without the presence germs. That means that other factors are also responsible for a person falling ill. Several factors are related to development of illness, such as stress, coping style, and change of climate.

Stress

Every now and then in our routine life we come across many problems. We try to know the seriousness of the problem and determine whether we have the emotional resources to deal with the problem. When the problem is serious for which we do not have the necessary resources to solve it, we perceive ourselves as being under stress. Stress is a process in which environmental demands strain an individual resulting in both psycological as well as biological changes pushing that a person at risk for illness. The things that cause stress are called *stressors*. Examples of *stressors* include earthquakes, divorce,

image tarnishing, and many more. More important the

goal is, more stressful a person would feel when that goal is threatened. So for example, if a person is to attend an interview, more of stress would be fet in case of traffic jam. Such a person is likely to feel more stress on the day of the interview in the traffic jam than any other day.

In a common man's life other *stressors* also include lack of job satisfaction, sexual harassment, discrimination, job security, domestic responsibilities, poor lighting and ventilation, pollution, noise, tension, depression, anxiety, criticism from friends and family members, domestic disputes, love affairs, heat, cold, frustration and many more so to say. Stress may be cognitive, emotional, physical or behavioural because one feels tense with complaints of aches, pains, diarrhea, constipation, nausea, dizziness and rapid heart palpitation. All these stresful conditions lead to illness.

Stress is not always considered a bad thing as certain amount is natural. No one lives without stress. Some amount of stress is normal while the chornic negative stress prolonging for long term is harmful for health. It is asserted that any change is stressful as it forces individuals to adapt to new, unfamilar circumstances. Some changes require more of an adjustment than other changes. For example the positive change resulting from wedding or promotion, and negative from divorce or unemployment are stressful which harm an individual's health.

When an individual is faced with stress, his body mobilises into action what is called fight or flight reaction. In such a process, the heartbeat increases, breathing gets accelerated, making the muscles tense. Another example is when apporoached by a thief, you can either fight him or try to run away from him. When an individual identifies a threat, activity in the sympathetic nervous system rises. Here peculiar hormones are released by the adrenaline glands because of which the nervous system and harmonal activity causes digestion to stop blood sugar levels from rising followed by the heart pumping more blood to the muscles. All of these reactions are not unlike the physiological aspects of strong emotions such as fear and anger.

Even after the initial fight or flight reaction if the stress persists then the body's reaction enters a second stage. During this stage the activity of the sympathetic nervous system declines. Hence, the stress continues and the body is unable to cope with likely breakdown of bodily resources causing reduction of the specific hormones in the brain, leading to severe depression. Stressful life events are certainly related to the risk of infected individuals developing an illness. The behavioural or biological processes contributing to the on set of disease are triggered by the traumatic stressful events. Chronic stress has been associated with increased reports of illness and the long-term exposure of chronic stress causes prolonged illness. It has been abserved that those who had either a work related or even interpersonal chronic *stressors* lasting one month or longer had increased risk of developiny colds as compared to those who had no chronic *stressor*. The longer the process endured, the more likely a person was to become ill. The psychological stress predicts a greater expression of illness.

Frequent climatic changes play a vital role in developing stress of any kind. Winter makes the skin dry, summer causes dehydration, autumn gives unpleasant feelings whereas monsoon brings water-borne diseases and the mosquitoes. The changes in climate make the movements restricted causing sizeable stress and ultimately leading to one or the other illness. Simply stress, not with standing germs can make a person ill.

Chapter 18
Techniques to bust your stress

Let it go. While we are upset we hold our breath; and releasing the breath is the basic form of letting go. It takes time say two to three minutes, in which you breath deeply and exhale. By closing your eyes, imagine your stress going away. Every time you exhal it will have calming effect.

You can cope with the emotional tensions by

It really works thereby relieving the pressure of stress quickly.

Make a list of your problems. Narrow the choices to minimum possible and tackle the most serious part

reduce considerly. If you are confused then focus on your problem continuously for about ten to eleven minutes. Don't get lost anywhere. Concentrating on one thing would certainly make you calmer fetching you good results in short time. This is a superb technique which you can do at workplace, home or anywhere.

While you are on your bed at night you can imagine visiting someone or places of amusement with birds. You would feel relaxed. You can repeat this technique during day time also. It would reduce your stressful moments.

- Try to be humble simple and polite which bring you peace of mind. You should always inculcate a habit such acts so as to get rid of emotional complications. If you are soft spoken then the stress would tend to be away from you.
- Keep on repeating a particular word in your mind may be religious or otherwise. Concentrating on a particular thing reduces stress. It is just a sort of meditation.
- Music is called a good transqiliser. It takes away the thoughts of anxiety from brain. In many hospitals light music is played in operation theatre as it produces calming effect on the patient before the operation is conducted. Even singing a song or dancing is good way of overcoming stress.
- You can reduce tension through movement which means walking, doing exercise or playing etc.
- Massage is extremely effective to overcome stress. It is a highly relieves stiff mucles. It is not necessary that you need a massager but you can do self massage too on some parts of your body.
- Your demands should not be unrealistic or unreasonable. Your expectations should be within your limits of competence and capability.
- Don't get stressed for having lost anything. Always remind yourself that whatever you lost will probably be available once again.
- You have to go for self apprisal to know your mistakes responsible for your stress.
- Don't dream of doing big things at once. You have to do everything gradually. So to say to climb the mountains first practice on hills. If you try to climb the mountains you are certainly going to fall.
- You should do things of your choice that your concious allows to avoid any stress.

- You should set easily attainable goal so that you can do that without putting hard efforts.
- Aim at reducing the unpleasent feelings when it seems difficult to relax. Once you reduce the tension slightly you would be able to overcome the stress gradually.
- Always have company of a good companion.
- Think of something you did very well giving yourself some appreciation.
- Enjoy a warm bath and watch a hilarious movie.
- Tell jokes and tease someone in a friendly way.
- Hug a friend impulsively.
- Play with your children's toys.
- Wear outrageous clothing.
- Be forgiving. Forgivness gives you feeling of inner satisfaction of mind. You are infact removing yourself away from the very causes of that hurt while you are forgiving someone. But if you carry on retaining a sense of revenge, you remain in stress.
- Be empathetic. Think of others and see the world standing in the other person's shoes. You will be able to see a thing in the correct perspective only by seeing the things from another person's eyes. While you look at the problems of other you would feel that you are in a much better situation.
- Be honest and generous. Honesty is not just about money. It is also about thoughts.
- You should be ready to admit mistakes. If you accept your faults you are not only improving yourself but also relieving yourself of the burden of carrying on the mistakes.
- Do not indulge in petty thoughts.
- Instead of rejoicing in the defeat of other people it would be better if you try to help them. That way your self esteem would rise and thereby reducing your stress.

- ❏ Don't get irritated over minor things.
- ❏ Don't have complicated thoughts. Try to simplify your thinking.
- ❏ Don't expect too much from others. By doing so, we only make ourselves miserable.
- ❏ Do what you have to do. Don't keep the expectations lingering in your mind.
- ❏ Laughter is a good medicine and considered a good stress buster. Do not be so serious. Laughing will relieve you of all troubles and completely destress you.

www.ingramcontent.com/pod-product-compliance
Lightning Source LLC
Chambersburg PA
CBHW070335230426
43663CB00011B/2321